791.4572

Grumpy Old Couples

Grumpy Old Couples

Jenny Eclair and Judith Holder

Illustrations by Ruth Murray

Weidenfeld & Nicolson
London

First published in Great Britain in 2008
by Weidenfeld & Nicolson

An Hachette Livre UK Company

10 9 8 7 6 5 4 3 2 1

Text © Jenny Eclair and Judith Holder 2008
Illustrations © Ruth Murray 2008

A CIP catalogue record for this book is available from the British Library.

ISBN 978 0 297 85364 0

Designed by Gwyn Lewis

Printed and bound in Great Britain by Mackays of Chatham plc, Chatham, Kent

Weidenfeld & Nicolson
The Orion Publishing Group Ltd
Orion House, 5 Upper Saint Martin's Lane
London, WC2H 9EA

www.orionbooks.co.uk

The Orion Publishing Group's policy is to use papers that are natural, renewable
and recyclable products and made from wood grown in sustainable forests. The
logging and manufacturing processes are expected to conform to the environ-
mental regulations of the country of origin.

Dedicated to couples who manage to stick together
for longer than is strictly necessary

Acknowledgements

Thanks to Lucy Jolly for her help in editing and putting the book together.

With loving thanks to Jean Holder.

And thanks to our two Grumpy Old Men, Mike Parker and Geof Powell

Contents

Introduction 9

1 Men are from Mars, women have just got back from Tesco's 13

2 Flirting 30

3 Courting or becoming a couple in the first place 53

4 Passion (or maybe not ...) 85

5 Grumpy old weddings 107

6 Resignation: the rot sets in 133

7 Despair 179

Introduction

We were asked to write a book about relationships, not because we're any good at them (we are decidedly bad at them) but because as self-appointed Head Girls of Grumpy Old Women, having done all the TV shows and co-written the live stage show together ... someone in trendy publishing-land thought we might have one or two grumpy things to say about relationships. We gave it a whirl, started jotting down some of the things that irritate us both about the whole business of lurve and relationships and, frankly, once we got going there was no stopping us. We had to be prized away from our laptops in the end. In fact I virtually wore out the keyboard on hers, and Jenny's still has the teeth marks to show for all the gnashing and teeth grinding involved.

Fortunately the publishers didn't want a self-help guide on how to get relationships right, nor a cute little book to put on your sweetheart's pillow on Valentine's Day, nor did they ask us to write a raunchy little number on how to be hot stuff in bed – which is just as well since neither of us would have known where to begin.

No, they wanted a book celebrating, or luxuriating in or wallowing in the almighty flipping minefield which is relationships with the opposite sex – or indeed in some cases same sex. Luckily both Jenny and I have been in our respective long-term relationships for a very very very

very long time, so let's just say that romance has turned to tolerance and idealism has turned to a quiet and sensible realisation that long-term relationships are more about being able to put up with one another, and being able to make the best of a bad job than managing to stay madly in love. Depressing? Not really, just realistic and anyway they both have incredibly patient partners who will read this and (hopefully) laugh, and let's face it both Jenny and I – like most middle-aged women – have hidden depths and many gorgeous and mysterious qualities that far outweigh superficial beauty or youth or glamour or sexual smouldering, none of which lasts in a relationship.

This book is about the grumpy aspects of having a partner, someone who has seen us looking both our best and our worst, who has made us chicken soup when we have been feeling unwell and with whom we from time to time shared bodily fluids. Living with a special friend (as I sometimes like to call them) is, as we both know, very challenging. They knock the top of their boiled eggs with a silly spoon action, they leave the top off biros by the kitchen phone and they dump their shoes just where you are likely to trip over them ... Yet having a special friend is often preferable to not having a special friend. Who else would you moan to at the end of the day when things have gone horribly wrong? Who else is going to help you do all those little jobs, and run into town for the second time when you have forgotten the double cream?

But in order for long-term relationships to last, you have to be able to let off steam, and so this book we hope will facilitate this, help us all to have one big group grump about living with your other half ... Face it, it's either read this book or reach for the omelette pan to thump them when he or she forgets to put the bin liner in the bin again. Think of it as a public service.

Equally, this book is a work of solidarity, a way of sharing the impossibly difficult nature of staying with your special friend for longer than it takes to find out how irritating they are. You might buy it for your own special friend, or you might know someone who is currently looking for a new special friend, or someone who has just been dumped by a special friend, or who is about to embark on a lifetime with their special friend, then hopefully this book will be a form of therapy. Think of it as permission to be grumpy about romantic entanglements in all their shapes and sizes.

Judith Holder

When Judith said we'd been asked to write a book about relationships, I sniggered, despite having lived with the same man for over a quarter of a century (he stole my youth). I'm the world's least romantic, hard-bitten, cynical old witch – ah, but I still expect presents on our anniversary, Valentine's Day and 'just because'!

Like most women I regard myself as an easy-going, kind-hearted, cheerful type. Well I would be if I didn't have to put up with him – the old fool – getting under my feet, wrapping apple cores in a tissue and then stashing them in a dirty coffee cup – give me strength – and generally making my life harder than it need be. But of course there's a flip side to everything. OK, he drives me mad and the last time I cried, because I was so tired and stressed from work, he smacked me on the bum and said, 'You'll be alright porker.' But seriously, when the chips are down it's good to have someone to ... well someone to blame really!

Although this book is mostly about man/woman relationships, it's also about all the other relationships that orbit your life and crash in on your everyday business. The poet John Donne once said 'No man is an island.' This is true. However, some people can afford to buy an island and get away from all the people that drive you bonkers.

That said, I'm glad I'm not lonely. I might be fed up to the back teeth, he might be getting on my nerves to the point where if we were married I'd want a divorce (yes, he's never bothered to make an honest woman out of me – can't blame him, I'd make a ghastly bride). But despite all this, I have to admit, I'm glad he's around, though obviously not all the time! Everyone needs a break now and again – which is why men must play golf.

As Judith has said, this is not a self-help book, God forbid. We do not advocate any healing crystals, chanting or feng shui, though personally I do believe in emptying your waste-paper baskets; not for any personal growth clap trap – it is just that brimming waste-paper baskets make the place look untidy and we're far too grumpy not to get cross about that.

So Grumpy Old Men, Grumpy Old Women, Grumpy Old Gays, unite. None of us are perfect – it's just some of us get closer to perfection than others!

Jenny Eclair

1 · Men are from Mars, women have just got back from Tesco's

Men and women are different. Get over it. Tragically God designed things so that both sexes are programmed to be physically, emotionally and intellectually poles apart, but he also designed us to need each other's sperm and egg and (most vitally) someone to hold the bottom of the ladder when we're trying to get the Xmas decorations down from the attic. This means that many of us are required to spend a large chunk of our lives living with an alien life force – which is perhaps God's idea of a practical joke.

Some people manage to remain a couple for longer than is strictly necessary – for twenty, thirty, forty years and more! The Queen and Prince Philip have notched up sixty years, despite the fact that his nickname for her is 'sausage', which, when she's feeling really grumpy is surely grounds for chopping off his head.

God, it must be great being the Queen. Any time he steps out of line she can have him sent to the Tower. If only the rest of us had the same privileges; heads would be rolling all over the place.

Let's face it, it's not easy being a couple and it's tougher being a Grumpy Old Couple. That's because everything's harder to deal with when you've got varicose veins and life seems to have turned into one enormous ingrowing toe-nail.

Surely couples who stay together for longer than say a quarter of a century should be rewarded by the government: medals should be dished out on silver and gold anniversaries, and maybe vouchers that could be exchanged for a mini cruise around the Mediterranean. Come on, it's the least we deserve. After all, it's not like having a long-term relationship with a member of the opposite sex is easy.

THE PROBLEM OF COMPATIBILITY

Men and women are wired differently ... for instance, as if any proof were needed ...

Men like women because they think women are the most amazing incredible thing on God's earth, whereas women tend to like men because chocolate can't mow the lawn. GUY BROWNING

The presumption is that men are brutes who just want relentless sexual gratification whereas women want to be taken round in horse-drawn carriages in a frock coat. STUART MACONIE

Women like (lots of) shoes, men like (lots of) sex
Women say the word 'shopping' and a man hears 'shoe shops'
Men say the words 'early night' and women hear 'a quickie'
Women say the words 'tidying up' and a man hears the words
    'mother-in-law coming to stay'
Men hear the word 'holiday' and they think 'bikini'
Women hear the word 'holiday' and they think 'diet'
Women need to talk, men would prefer to be doing Su Doku
Women want the lawn mown, men want to sit on it
Women know the difference between a 70c wash and a
    40c colour wash
Men leave their pants and socks on the floor
Men can't make a bed properly
Men can't do anything properly
Men have perfected selective hearing, especially when a woman
    'needs to talk'
Napkins do not figure in a man's life (unless he is gay), women
    like them on the table
Men don't understand why *Heat* magazine is important
Men are good at general knowledge quizzes in pubs, women cheat
Men can shave their hairy chins quickly and efficiently with an
    electric razor, women must pluck, pluck, pluck
Men fart and say ' better out than in'
Women 'let off' and say 'it's only wind'
A man can go to the supermarket and come out with a single tub
    of ice cream, which he will then proceed to eat in the car
A woman will pop into the supermarket, pick up a basket and
    then remember that everyone needs lavatory paper and
    while she's at it she might as well get emergency batteries,
    candles, a jar of piccalilli, some antiseptic wipes, a cauli-
    flower and a new nutmeg grater ... eventually, by the time
    she gets the trolley through the check-out, she will have
    spent £300 on groceries, which is more than that nice pair
    of boots she had her eye on in Hobbs

Women paint their toe-nails; not even Russell Brand does this

Men will dollop brown sauce all over their breakfast Men are from Mars, women have just got back from Tesco's *à la* Jackson Pollock, women go for a neat little dipping blob

Men like cricket; women are scared of that hard red leather ball smacking them in the mouth and taking out their teeth and think 'the audience' at cricket matches should be offered free dental shields

Men don't call people who go and watch a cricket match 'the audience'

Only gay men and women like musicals, although straight men sometimes inadvertently hum show tunes

Men, however, will make an exception to see the musical *Chicago* – this might have something to do with fishnet stockings

Women don't understand *The Bourne Identity*, men don't understand *Hollyoaks*

Men watch *Top Gear* because they are interested in cars, women watch *Top Gear* because they fancy Richard Hammond

Women instinctively know who you are talking about when you say 'Fern and Philip', men think you might be referring to that couple you got chatting to on the hovercraft over to Calais last year

Men think it might be a good idea to stock up on cheap booze in France, women think it would be nice to have a romantic weekend in Paris

Men think bringing the Mrs breakfast in bed on her birthday is a nice thing to do, women wish he didn't bother – in fact it gets the day off to a really bad start, especially when he's gone and put milk in your tea when you haven't drunk milk in your tea for twenty-five years! The idiot

Women keep babies' booties and their children's first teeth, men keep rusty hinges and old cans of paint

Men really can get a bus through there

Men speak in sentences, women speak in paragraphs – or at
   certain times of the month in chapters
Men don't notice or appreciate or even see cushions or curtains
Men have the capacity to sleep though most sounds, whether it
   is a dog barking or a doorbell ringing – and especially a baby
   crying
Women have an ability to make men think they are really in charge
If you told a woman you had just returned from a trip to Mars
   the only thing she'd be interested in is who you'd gone with

So, how was it ever meant to work?

WHAT ARE MEN LOOKING FOR IN A WOMAN?

*I think men until they find the right person are just looking for
someone they can have good sex with and who won't get in the
way too much.*   MARIELLA FROSTRUP

Physically

Men like women with big boobs and look like they might be fun
in bed ... More specifically, according to research done by people
who have nothing better to do, men go for women who look like
they ENJOY sex, and apparently men spend some time speculating
mentally what women would look like when they orgasm, which is
a bit scary. And women assume, apparently wrongly as it turns
out, that men decide whether to sleep with them primarily according to how skinny or fat they are. So, instead of spending weeks
at WeightWatchers, we should all be doing a When Harry Met Sally
or a Paris Hilton, which also explains why so many young women
go clubbing in dresses the size of face flannels leaving nothing to
the imagination – something Grumpy Old Women strongly disapprove of. What a good job we are no longer out on the pull on a
Saturday night.

The rest of what men are after is more practical ...

Men are looking for someone who will answer the telephone,
    organise Christmas and preferably not be too stingy with
    the gravy
A man wants a woman who will keep things that he might need
    in her handbag: a biro, spare keys to his bicycle lock, local
    train timetable, some toffees, his inhaler/heart pills/
    artificial sweeteners

Fact

It is entirely possible that if men had learnt to carry handbags they
wouldn't need a woman and the human race would die out completely. But most of all, men want women to make them look clever
and powerful and manly, which is fine as long as they haven't just
had to call the AA out to help them change a tyre because it was
raining a bit, or ask you to unblock the drain under the sink because
the gunge in it makes them feel sick. Sometimes men can be such
girls.

WHAT ARE WOMEN LOOKING FOR IN A MAN?

*Women are still looking for someone who will be supportive of
them and take care of them and be strong. When I say supportive
I don't necessarily mean financially. But they also want them to
be drop dead gorgeous, great in bed, devilish naughty and faithful,
so it's no wonder that so many women spend a long time looking
for Mr Right.*   MARIELLA FROSTRUP

*There's no politically correct way of saying this, but ladies are
romantic, gentlemen tend not to be romantic. Gentlemen that fail
to understand this are doomed.*   LAURENCE LLEWELYN-BOWEN

Women like men whom other women find attractive
They like men who will buy them nice things
They like a nice smile or a friendly fatherly wink
They like a man who has a shower every day
They like a man who says, 'Don't worry your pretty head about
that, I will deal with it', and then deals with it
They like a man who knows where the mains water tap is

In other words, women are quite shallow, in an endearingly charming sort of way. And men are quite selfish ... which amounts to the same thing really.

What women don't look for in a man:

Names of other ladies tattooed all over his torso
Dandruff and dirty nails (unless he's got a really macho oily job
like racing-car mender)
Bankruptcy
A gambling addiction
A thing about all the towels being straight in the bathroom
(listen, if anyone's going to have ocd in the house then it's
the woman's prerogative)
Story-telling (as in lying)
Someone who has ever featured on *The Jeremy Kyle Show/
Crimewatch/Britain's Got Talent* (and done really badly)
A stupidly large willy

What men don't look for in a woman:

Bossiness (but tough we say)
Food issues
Hang-ups about taking clothes off
Hang-ups about keeping clothes on
Non gravy maker
Someone who likes karaoke, even though she shouldn't

Mooning tendencies, i.e. breasts out on big dipper or bum out on
    back seat of coach
Serious soap addiction – all the usuals plus the duds: *Emmerdale*,
    Doctors and *Neighbours*
Kleptomania
Ball breakers both metaphorically and literally

WHY BOTHER WITH THE WHOLE MR & MRS MALARKEY?

The only reason that women put up with men is a) they want babies
and b) they are rubbish at technology and once the kids have left
home they need someone to show them how to programme the
microwave or change a SIM card. It's not that women are stupid,
they just find it tiresome and can't be bothered, and if they are
smart about it they get men to do it for them by pretending men are
cleverer than us. Ha!

It's not like it's just confined to technology. Here are some
more things that are too technical, disgusting or dull for a woman
to do and therefore are 'jobs for the boys':

Putting oil in the car
Taking all 'that stuff' to the tip
Lagging the boiler
Bleeding radiators
Picking up a dead mouse
Changing a ball cock in the loo
Securing a Catherine Wheel safely to a wall
Bringing the Xmas tree into the house
Changing and being responsible for all light bulbs
Leaf sweeping and checking of guttering – i.e. removing tennis
    balls from drains
Pond maintenance
Annual cleaning of barbecue

Don't tell men this but their jobs are much harder than our jobs – this is a secret us women must take to the grave. In the meantime we must create as much myth as possible about the difficulties of female domesticity, even if all you ever do is hide rubbish under the bed and drink coffee with your mates – shhhhhhhhhhhh.

The only reason that men put up with women is:

They need someone to bring them boiled eggs and soldiers when they have a cold
They like blow-jobs

Some other things that men need women to do for them:

Buy Xmas presents for all their living relatives
Choose holiday destinations, thereby bearing all guilt if it goes wrong; also, once on holiday being solely responsible for the purchase and application of factor 25 sunscreen for all family members
Act as speaking diary and remind him on a daily basis about dental/medical appointments/drinks with the lads/congestion charge payment/*Spooks* being on the telly
Leave a note for the cleaner
Remember which beds need changing this week
Scratch the bits they can't reach

WHAT ATTRACTS US TO ONE ANOTHER IN THE FIRST PLACE

Men really do seem to be rather hung up on something as superficial as looks. They fancy someone looks-wise first and then are attracted (or not) to their personality, whereas research shows that women are often attracted to men's personality (or car) before their looks, and that looks are generally much less important.

To put it another way, clearly men are shallow and women are mature and full of depth and wisdom. This would also explain why George Clooney continues to be more and more attractive the older and greyer (and more distinguished) he gets, whereas ageing female superstars like Brigitte Bardot are thought of as wrinkly old prunes. Trouble is women then spoil it all by being attracted to men's money and power – which is surely the only possible explanation for why men like Peter Stringfellow manage to attract young good-looking women. Clearly there should be a law against this. We say men like Peter Stringfellow should be made to sleep with a woman of his own age ... like Ann Widdecombe.

Even physically there is a mismatch between the sexes ... Men like big boobs, but women don't because they like to be able to jiggle about without a bra sometimes and anyway big boobs get in the way when you roll over in bed. Jordan is a precautionary tale: she enlarged her petite figure with so much silicone that it's incredible that she can actually sit close enough to her keyboard in order to type those bestselling books of hers, but maybe she's got very long arms.

Ideally men would like a harem. One woman isn't really sufficient, unless she's a big-boobed, gravy-making, soft hearted sex siren – preferably with a twin sister.

And while we're on the subject of the old ménage-à-trois: remember, if a man badgers you for a threesome, only give in on the proviso that it's a two -man, one -woman combination and see how quickly he goes off the idea!

Some women like to con themselves that a nice personality and a pleasant smile are enough to pull a bloke. Unfortunately they aren't – and woe betide the woman who has too much personality. Men are very suspicious of 'funny' women; they secretly think it's a fine line between being 'funny' and being a bit nutty.

Teenage girls are quick to realise this. There are thousands of teenage girls who play the class clown at their girls-only schools, only to become mute sycophants as soon as boys come into the equation. These are the clever ones. The girls who continue to pull stupid faces and make farting noises are the ones that boys steer clear of.

Nothing spoils a romance so much as a sense of humour in
a woman. OSCAR WILDE

Women – on the other hand – are attracted much more to a man's personality/shoes/car/voice than they are to just his physique. They look beyond the physical package – and a man who is say follicly challenged but oozing with charm and personality can be extremely successful with women, especially if they drive a nice car or have one of those swish flats with a cream sofa and marble tops in the kitchen (then again that might mean they're gay). Women are attracted by someone who shows signs that they will offer them reassurance, who they feel an affinity to, who makes them laugh, understands them, and let's be honest knows what makes women orgasm. The last bit is quite important by the way. Some men only have a very vague idea, in which case get a grip and read some manuals. It's not rocket science, well OK it is a bit, but if you're over twenty-five there is no excuse at all.

If only we could be more scientific in our approach to choosing partners, if only 'fancying' them or not fancying them wasn't such a lottery.

OK, let's just apply some logic. For example, a small woman should marry a tall man; that way, when they go shopping, he can reach the things that she needs off the top shelf. A fat man should have a thin wife, but not one who is so thin he could roll over and squash her in bed. Posh people should only go out with posh people, otherwise that 'weak chin' thing will filter through all the other classes and there will be far too many little girls called Camilla.

As a rule inter-class relationships should be avoided. The middle classes need to stick together as no-one else can stand their smugness and their incessant talk about schools. As for the working class, they should keep to their own, or else there will be daily arguments over having milk cartons on the table and saying 'settee'.

Unfortunately when love walks into the room logic flies out of the window and the most unsuitable types get together.

Of course any relationship can survive as long as the couple communicate – ha ... This is easier said than done.

Men don't do communication. It's not their thing, it's not their fault, it's not their problem. If mother nature had intended a man to show his emotions, she'd have put his knob in the middle of his face. JENNY ECLAIR

TALKING

Women need to talk more than anything else. Words are our drug; we need them as much as we need chocolate and oxygen. Women like to talk about everything, and they especially like to talk about their relationship. On the other hand, men don't like to talk much at all. They can happily stand at a bus stop without saying, 'Well this is ridiculous, twenty minutes I've been standing here. I will have to write a letter.' Men would rather rinse out a chemical lavvy than talk about their relationship. This leads to great grumpiness.

Men are happy when they are watching sport or trying to put a little white ball in a hole the size of a ping-pong ball from a distance of half a mile, and will do anything to avoid talking about anything 'important' emotionally. So, whilst women are happy when they are talking about emotional stuff over a glass of dry white wine, men constantly go in for distraction tactics. Fortunately women are not easily distracted when we are talking and so we carry on, trying to make sense of everything, talking it through and generally chewing the cud. Men sometimes make the mistake of trying to talk back to women who are mid cud chewing, which is not what women want at all, and yet more grumpiness occurs.

Women want to talk, talk it out, talk it right through – they've got to flat-line with their conversation, they want to go right the way down to the end and then come right the way back up again and then they're fine. You haven't actually said anything. All you've done is gone 'yeah yeah yeah'. Let them flat-line. They just want you to listen. You can be thinking about the football – anything – doesn't matter. Just nod.   BRIAN CONLEY

The other thing where you can never go wrong with women is to listen to what they're saying and nod. You don't have to listen but you just have to nod and eventually they will say, 'Well what do you think', and all you have to say because you won't have been listening is, 'I think we need to talk' because they love that. So you don't have to listen, you just have to say, 'I think we need to talk' and then you get more talk that you don't have to listen to, and as long as women are talking they think they're actually in control of the situation, so as long as you can keep listening you're fine.
GUY BROWNING

The truth is (and don't tell them this) women actually like talking to men. In some respects it's better than talking to women, because girlfriends interrupt, pretend to be sympathetic, then give you some half-baked advice and then as soon as you have paused for breath, leap in and expect you to listen to all their dreary tales of domestic woe, like how 'Gordon keeps mixing up the recycling boxes and can't seem to tell the difference between plastic and paper' – yawn.

The great thing about talking to men is that because they don't really listen they can't remember what you actually said. This means that when you accidentally contradict yourself (like all the time) he doesn't even notice ... the fool.

Men are getting away with more and more when it comes to listening – or rather less and less. Technology is on their side, what with these newfangled mini iPods with their weeny earphones. With clever positioning of a scarf and covering the ears with either a hat or hair, us girls don't even realise that instead of hanging onto our every word our menfolk are in fact listening to Bob Dylan or the sports results.

Men will often make the mistake of cutting off completely from the sound of a woman's voice; they just tune out. This is very, very annoying, especially when they have perfected a 'lalala not listening' sort of face for when her 'wittering' is getting on his nerves. Women can spot this face a mile off and it's maddening.

BEING A COUPLE AGAINST ALL ODDS

Despite men and women having nothing in common and not even listening to each other, despite the fact that we can buy and sell eggs and sperm on the internet, men and women are still 'getting it on'.

Why? Because oddly enough men and women are good together, like cheese and pickle, ice cream and jelly and sausage and mustard.

Why men and women are good together

He can answer all the questions about war on *Who Wants to be a Millionaire*, she knows who Isabella Rossellini is

He knows where to put the oil into the car, which means it doesn't break down when she goes to pick him up from the pub

He knows how to use a power drill, she knows where he put it

She knows when the lawn needs mowing, he knows when mowing it will make his life worth living

She can spend ten minutes parking in a tricky space, he can come and rescue her when she can't get out of it

He can be relied on to order chips, she can be relied on to eat at least seven

The fact is, your dog may be very well trained but he cannot fetch a toilet roll from the cupboard under the stairs when you have been caught short – a man can ... just about.

WHAT ARE WE LOOKING FOR IN A PARTNER?

Someone to fill in our tax return form

Someone who knows how to make a bed or can pick you up from the airport at three in the morning without making a great song and dance about it

We also expect birthdays and anniversaries to be remembered, help taking off our Wellington boots, someone to share that bottle of wine (or we'll drink the whole bloody lot), a familiar face to sit opposite in a nice restaurant, and the occasional compliment

We all want love, we all want to know that there is someone special out there who one day will want to involve us in expensive legal problems, cut all our clothes up, condense our life down to bin bags ... (let it go Jeff).   JEFF GREEN

Romance

Women are looking for romance, men find it hard to define what romance is.

Personally I think the definition of romantic is very straight forward: romantic is anything, any gesture, any present, any object that inspires Mrs Llewelyn-Bowen to raise her nightie.
LAURENCE LLEWELYN-BOWEN

Again we have a fundamental difference between the sexes. On the whole women are more romantic than men but men have cleverly realised it's in their best interest to acknowledge and demonstrate romance within a relationship.

Women tend to remember dates. This is from years spent working out when they last had a period and hoping they're not pregnant. Hence women will remember birthdays and anniversaries, whereas men only remember dates such as 30 July 1966 when England won the World Cup.

There are good and bad types of romance.

Bad romance is:

Poor quality chocolate

A badly made teddy bear with synthetic fur holding a red satin heart-shaped cushion embroidered with the words 'I love you', or 'for someone special'

Flowers from the Shell garage

The word romantic to me means sloppy.   MATTHEW PARRIS

Good romance is:

Unstacking the dishwasher even when it isn't their turn

Making you chicken soup when you are poorly

Mending a shirt and making sure the thread is the same colour as the shirt

It's about the little things and it's about responding to who they are and what you know they'll enjoy, and if that's a bunch of flowers then fantastic. But it could just as easily be taking the rubbish out.   KATHRYN FLETT

Romantic gestures

Of course some people go overboard on the romance stakes. If you ask me, there are far too many sheets hung over railway bridges saying 'Kelly I love you' and embarrassing proposals on live television (this is particularly worrying when it happens on *Trisha Goddard* or *Jeremy Kyle*).

Whatever you do, don't think buying her a single red rose from some illegal immigrant in a dodgy Italian restaurant constitutes romance. It doesn't. Flowers can actually backfire, oddly enough. Women don't like massive bouquets complete with weird-shaped stick things that might just take your eye out .We never have a big enough vase and you end up fighting with your flowers rather than arranging them. As with most things, if you don't really know what you're doing, keep it simple.

Of course women vary in their attitudes to romance.

Jenny on the one hand is a complete contradiction when it comes to soppiness. Despite being a hard-faced old boot, she can be suprisingly mawkish.

> *I can sob buckets over babies being born. That gets me every time but I've got a very low threshold for a rom com – think I've got a lot of testosterone in me as I'd rather watch* Fight Club *than* Breakfast at Tiffany's. *JENNY ECLAIR*

Judith on the other hand started crying the moment *Love Actually* started, with that scene of people saying goodbye to people they love at Heathrow Airport, and cried all the way through (with the exception of the soft porn scenes). She came out with a handful of sopping wet tissues and looking like she had walked into a plate-glass window. Having said that, she is not very good at being romantic herself and expects her spouse to be very very romantic indeed. Which is not fair. But then love is not very fair, is it?

To summarise the differences between men and women:

women want – money and babies
men want – sex and praise

Oh dear. No wonder we end up as Grumpy Old Couples.

2 · Flirting

How do two polemically different species ever manage to get together at all? Answer – they get a little bit drunk, or 'bladdered', as the young people so elegantly put it nowadays, and they start flirting with one another. The latest disturbing news on the binge-drinking craze is that teenagers, and young women in particular, are drinking so much that their bladders are actually bursting, This is not an urban myth, this is true – not on my carpet young lady.

Let's just sort something out before we go any further. You don't need to be drunk to flirt, not when you're grown-up and not during the day (unless you're at a wedding when it's de rigueur and you're allowed to flirt with someone a good deal younger than you).

The scary thing is that you know whether you fancy someone almost instantly. Apparently someone has done scientific experiments and they have discovered that most people take between ninety seconds and four minutes to decide if they fancy someone (but about thirty years to make sure).

The trouble with this statistic is that, while you might know that you fancy someone from the moment they step foot on the bus, how do you know whether they're available/not mad/gay...? Basically, at this point you must begin a process of elimination and it all starts with flirting. First of all you need to catch their eye. This is quite easy, unless of course they realise they've got on the wrong bus and jump off at the next stop without noticing that you even exist – drat ... he/she could have been 'the one'.

Whatever you do, do not jump off the bus and follow them. Sometimes it's just not meant to be.

Some people are better than others at flirting. Some are born flirts, and usually they have long blonde hair that they flick about a lot, or if they are blokes they are tall and dark and handsome but tragically they flirt with other, more glamorous women than Jenny or Judith. So flirts – both male and female – are officially annoying. Flirting is the fun bit of getting to know the opposite sex, as long as you are not in competition with other women or men for someone's flirtatious attention, in which case it is very annoying indeed. But then the whole business of trying to pull is, on the whole, both stressful and tiring and, above all, deeply disappointing. How many times can you remember admiring someone say across a crowded room, and they have admired you back and made a b-line for you and you have ended up having a fabulously exciting relationship as a result? You can count those incidents possibly on one hand, or make that one finger, because most of the time, the one you fancy fancies someone else, or is already with someone else, and you end up going home with a late-night kebab or a special brew and some Doritos.

Of course gay men have got this sussed and they have a whole code of hankies hanging out of various pockets indicating availability and special sexual dietary requirements. Us straights should adopt our own code, especially ageing grumps who can't be doing with any 'time wasters'.

Basically what most people want to flag up is, I'm single, I'm not mad, I get a bit lonely and I'd like someone to share my life with.

Thing is, we tend to overcomplicate things.

Grumpy Old Women in particular can be quite demanding. It's not enough to find someone who is single, solvent and continent. No, we start raising the bar. We want stuff like a clean driving licence, evidence of recently flossed teeth and not only hair, but hair that smells nice. There aren't enough key and hankie combinations in the world that could possibly describe what it is we're after.

Frankly it would be so much simpler to be a gay man who is truly happy with a quickie round the back of a tree.

Being able to receive flirting signals accurately is as important as being able to send them, and of course when you are on the nursery slopes you can get them horribly wrong; some of us get them horribly wrong all our lives. Sometimes someone who you have known for five years, maybe worked with or travelled alongside for as long as you can remember, takes you utterly by surprise and says something provocative and you realise they have been flirting for years, or fancied you for years. Scary, but true. The trouble with flirting is that it's meant to be subtle – which can lead to misinterpretation. Flirting is a sort of foreign language, and occasionally things get lost in translation. Why can't people just come straight out with it and tell you whether they fancy you or not?

I can't bear people who flirt. It is the most ridiculous pursuit. If you are cooking someone a meal, would you hand a crisp to them and then pull it away before they could get it? Flirting is just a waste of time; people should put up or shut up.
MATTHEW PARRIS

I still enjoy flirting. I think flirting is very harmless; it's a sort of basic human need like brushing your teeth.   MARIELLA FROSTRUP

I'd prefer it if adult relationships were conducted like playground relationships used to be. I think it would be better if a woman fancies you she sends over a big mate to push you and say, 'Will you go out with my mate?' I think that the adult world would be much simpler if they did that instead of having to read these signs. STUART MACONIE

Of course, just as there are lots of gorgeous men and women who have no idea how utterly fanciable they are, there is an equal number of both men and women who, for some reason, think that the world can't wait to bed them. The trouble with confidence on this scale is that it can become a self-fulfilling prophecy – which is how the most dandruffy of men can end up getting off with something that looks like Sophia Loren's granddaughter. In the words of George Michael, 'You gotta have faith.'

Confidence in a man is very attractive, confidence in a woman can be off-putting for some blokes. Sometimes it's best to play the shoe-less waif in a snow storm. One of the tricks to flirting is being able to pretend to be something that you aren't. Say for example you're the female boss of a massive corporation, you're used to striding around shouting your head off and firing people. Well you can't be that person when you're trying to pull; you have to pretend to be the kind of woman that's too weak to open a heavy door.

Flirting should have been on the school curriculum. It would certainly have been more useful than physics or learning about vectors in maths, which was my personal cut-off point ... At the very least it should have been a badge at Scouts or Guides, instead of which we had to spend our lives floundering around trying to grasp some of the basics.

FLIRTING RULES FOR WOMEN

You have to wear heels – flatties or slippers are no-go

Having hair that is tied up in a bun that comes undone at a
    certain crucial moment is good

Hair in general is an aid to flirting, though oddly enough an
    attractive bald man's pate is a great flirt magnet, as women
    will want to stroke it or even rub it, like Buddha's tummy
    for luck

Fringes act as a sort of peekaboo flirty curtain – but probably
    only if you're Kate Moss. Judi Dench on the other hand has a
    no-nonsense, no-flirt fringe – sort of a Roundhead rather
    than a Cavalier fringe. Fact: the Cavaliers were sexier than
    the Roundheads – it's just one of those things – just as
    Italians are sexier than Germans (apart from Heidi Klum
    and Claudia Schiffer I suppose)

Lick your lips, but not so often that it looks like you are audition-
    ing for the part of the big bad wolf in a local panto

Bat your eyelashes, though this can get tiring and it can look like
    a facial tic; don't get obsessive though; don't start counting
    between 'bats'

Laugh at his jokes; don't sneer and say in a withering tone of
    voice 'haha, very funny not'

Pretend you can't open something; the back of your mobile
    phone is good, a massive jar of pickled onions, which you
    keep in your handbag for such occasions, is bad

Look impressed; men will believe anything that makes them
    feel good

Don't keep looking at your watch and yawning – even though
    you really want to

Don't sleep with him on the first date; OK, well not unless you
    really want to

FLIRTING RULES FOR MEN

Ask her some questions, but make sure they are personal and
not things like, 'What's the longest river in the world?' or
'Twenty points if you know what a campanile is?' (it's a
freestanding bell tower – the most famous example being
the Leaning Tower of Pisa)

Listen to her properly. Don't keep one eye on the telly in the
corner of the pub, not even if it's a crucial match on a
massive screen – say like the World Cup. Concentrate on
the job in hand

Don't call her 'Frannie', unless her name is 'Frannie'

Laugh at her jokes, but make sure what she's saying is meant to
be funny; it can be a very fine line with women

Tell her she smells nice but don't sniff her neck unless she
offers it to you

TYPES OF FLIRTS – WOMEN

The bubbly blonde

This one has to tread a very fine line between being 'good fun' and
the 'life and soul' and turning into an incoherent mess throwing up
on the night bus.

The sultry brunette

Does nothing, nothing at all, has no personality, doesn't speak,
socially the laziest lump of space waste, but men love her.
Why? She doesn't do anything apart from sit there looking a bit
miserable. I dunno, you blokes, we despair.

The up-for-anything slightly bonkers redhead

This is the girl who wears a black pvc mac with nothing on underneath. She will do anything she's dared to do. Men fancy her, but are
a bit scared of her.

The slightly over-the-hill flirt

Great from a distance, very scary close up. It's fine when she's winking and beckoning from the other side of the room; it's only when you venture over that you realise she has long yellow teeth like a horse and loads of broken purple veins around her nose.

TYPES OF FLIRTS – MEN

The fop

Styles himself entirely on Hugh Grant, all bumbling good manners and cut-glass accent. The ex-public school-boy flirt will play the little boy lost card quite a lot and inevitably, if you do end up in bed, he will wet it.

The cheeky chappy

Will wear a very tight white T-shirt because he's kept himself tidy, will make you laugh so much that your knickers fall off, you will have a great time but he will never remember your name in the morning.

The lovable rogue

Kisses everyone on the lips, even when it's highly inappropriate. For example, when the lovable rogue ends up in court, he will try to give the female magistrate a 'smacker', wears a sheepskin coat and keeps a hip flask of brandy 'for medicinal purposes' (and getting women drunk enough to sleep with him) in his back pocket. Has a tendency towards bigamy – but doesn't mean any harm.

The hopeless unemployed poet

Doesn't need to do anything apart from write poetry, forgets to shave/go to the dentist and looks sad – Irish accents are a bonus. Women flock to the dishevelled wreck; you think you can change him, make a success out of him. You can't.

The car flirt

Will have spent a fortune on a flirty sports car to flirt in. Unfortunately he will spend his entire life waiting to pull up next to a pretty girl at some traffic lights; with any luck this will never happen. Haha – you fool with your personalised number plate.

OUR PERSONAL TRACK RECORD ON FLIRTING

Jenny is and was a very successful flirt. Romance has never played a huge part in her relationships; she's just not very romantic. In the old days, when she fancied someone, it was never in a swooney kind of way, it was in a slightly competitive, let's go out and get him kind of way. She looked on potential love interest as 'prey'.

Because she was such a determined and focused flirter, Jenny was the kind of girl people like Judith dreaded being in competition with – forward, pushy, assertive and a bit common: a deadly and winning combination when it came to boys. Whereas Judith, as a teenager, was completely hopeless and clung on to even the most impossible relationship, even when it was obvious to all around that it was going nowhere – just to avoid further flirting.

Jenny was the sort of girl who would come and overtake on the outside lane, barge in at the youth club or on the playing fields and bag the boy in one swift move – probably just went straight up to him and snogged him. Maddening.

> *I remember when kiss chase used to turn into something David Attenborough would present on a wildlife documentary. You'd siphon off the weakest one – the boy who had one leg shorter than the other – head him off from the rest of the herd and run him up a blind alley. Later on I used the same sort of method in night-clubs. The trick is to dance them into a corner and then, when they're squashed up against a wall, go in for the kill.*
> JENNY ECLAIR

One big advantage Judith has (or *had* more accurately) is that Jenny wears glasses and frankly you can't flirt in glasses, and once you take your glasses off you have to be very careful what you flirt with because your quality control slips.

Warning

Removing glasses + alcohol + more alcohol = sleeping with someone who looks like they live under the carpet.

TRIAL AND ERROR

I suppose there is not much difference between flirting and showing off. Flirting is just showing off with sexual intent. Basically you're saying the same thing, 'Look at me, look at me, aren't I great? Love me, love me.' The trick is never to say these words out loud as this can be quite off-putting.

If only finding a mate was as easy as sidling up to someone you like the look of and saying, 'Hey you're a bit of alright, you are. How about we both go out for a bit and see if we really like one another?' Being so direct is for some reason a total no-no, the whole thing has to be subtle. I suppose the reason is obvious. Yes, you can obviously choose to go up to someone (and some of us tragically have) and say, 'Hey, I really fancy you, how about it?' But the chances are you will a) take them by surprise b) they will think you are bonkers or c) they will not fancy you and so you will be dumped with a capital D, as in huge emotional damage will ensue. The one big advantage after all of not doing the asking is that you run less risk of a damaging rejection.

This used to be one of the perks of being a girl: you never had to do the lonely walk across the dance floor in order to ask a person of the opposite sex to dance/go out with you. Nowadays girls are allowed to pick up boys, which means that they must do the lonely walk across the dance floor only to face the possibility of being laughed at by some bloke and all his mates. This is called equality – we call it revenge.

There is, I guess, some logic in taking things slowly, sending out and picking up little signals that get a little bit bolder and a little bit bolder each time until the next thing you know you're snogging and he wants to see you on Wednesday night. At this point you should be able to relax but, for some reason, this is when it gets even more complicated and people start playing games.

Some women work on the principle of 'treat them mean keep them keen'. But how do you know, if by treating 'em 'mean' you're going to cross some invisible line that makes him think, 'Actually she's a horrible cow and I don't want anything to do with her.' At which point he dumps her, she does loads of crying, her best mate tries to mediate, he fancies the best mate and the whole flirting cycle begins all over again.

Finding a partner is a mind-boggling process of trial and error, come-ons and rejections, which may explain why most successful flirting goes on in crowded, busy, loud places where frankly one's mistakes can go relatively unnoticed. Other advantages in using dark dingy nightclubs as pulling places include the fact that low lighting causes pupils to dilate – and there is a lot of scientific evidence that dilated pupils are a very strong unconscious signal to indicate that people are aroused, or fancy you. Scary.

WOOING AROUND THE WORLD

Flirting has been around for a very long time. In medieval Italy, for instance, women put belladonna (a poison) in their eyes to make them look bigger. (And bella donna translates as 'beautiful lady') ... the things we do for love. And we thought contact lenses were a pain in the neck.

In Niger, Woodaba tribesmen dress in feminine costumes during an annual festival to woo women. The young men, wearing jewels and make-up, dance in front of young female judges and the winning men are rewarded with 'a night of love with the judges'. Imagine – they had X Factor there first!

In Paraguay, when two women of the Chaco Indian tribe want to marry the same man, they don tapir-skin boxing gloves and fight it out (so what's new – they do the same in Sunderland).

The women of the Trobriand Islands near Papua New Guinea go up to the man of their choice and bite him on the arm (beats having to listen to their jokes).

In Ethiopia the males of the Surma tribe fight with phallic sticks in a courtship ritual (then presumably they get exported to Ann Summers).

Karo women in Ethiopia are considered more sexually attractive if they make deep cuts in their torsos and rub ash in them (even for George Clooney this might prove a step too far for most of us).

And of course in the UK, women spend hundred of pounds making themselves look gorgeous for Elaine's fortieth birthday party, get overexcited because they've had their eyebrows professionally groomed, have one glass of punch too many and fall asleep on the bathroom floor at 10 p.m.

SENDING OUT SIGNALS

In the past

Signals and flirting and the chase may seem convoluted, but they are positively brutal compared to how the whole business of courting was in Jane Austen's time. During the Victorian era, romantic love was the primary requirement for marriage and courting rituals were very formal. An interested gentleman could not walk up to a young woman and strike up a conversation – he had to be formally introduced and only after some time was it considered appropriate for him to speak to her or for the couple to be seen together.

Once formally introduced, if the man wanted to escort the woman home from a social function he would present his card to her, and at the end of the event she would review her options and choose her escort. She would then notify the man of her choice by giving him her own card requesting that he escort her home. I think we call these sales conferences nowadays.

Although there were rigid courting rules, it was easy to check out whether a fellow fancied you. You simply dropped your glove and, as long as he picked it up and returned it to you, you were as good as engaged. That's what we see in the movies anyway. What we never see is the glove being deliberately walked on and ground into the mud by a cad who is not remotely interested – which was of course the 18th-century equivalent of refusing to be someone's 'friend' on Facebook (which by the way is not something anyone over forty should be doing).

Body language

So much of this business of giving out signals is not about what you say at all, it's all in the body language, the way you look at someone – in fact only 7% of flirtatious communication is verbal.

> *I have absolutely no idea what signals I am sending people and I am not looking for people sending signals to me. There is no need to send signals; we're not at sea. People should just say something.*
> MATTHEW PARRIS

> *If you're sitting next to somebody and they start stroking the furniture beside you, that invariably means they are desperate to actually do that to you.*   TRACEY COX

The experts say to watch the feet of the person you're attracted to, because apparently where the toes point the heart follows, and people who are attracted to each other subconsciously try to 'line up' with the other person. Perhaps line dancing has its use then.

Flirting signals

Men send out the following signals when they're interested:

Smile
Extend eye contact
Groom (straighten their ties, pull up their socks)
Sit up or stand up straight
Stand with their chests thrust out and their shoulders back
    (like a preening peacock)
Make comments about their successes in life (jobs/cash/cars)
Put one hand in their pocket with a thumb sticking out, or tuck
    their thumbs in their belt; they are unwittingly highlighting
    their genitals by framing them in this way, and they are also
    saying this is their territory and they will defend it

As the woman approaches, the men exhibit more preening behaviour. They will usually have a 'flirting face', some will try to look a bit moody – this is to flag up the possibility that they are interesting and deep, that they've possibly been hurt in the past or maybe they're harbouring a secret, a secret that could cost lives. That's right, he's pretending to be a spy.

Whereas women:

Extend eye contact
Smile
Lean forward or towards you
Expose their neck, hands or palms
Flip their hair about or twirl it
Cross and uncross their legs
Wet their lips – either by licking them or with lip gloss
Fondle cylindrical objects like wine-glass stems, pens or
    cigarettes; unless she's in the porn industry, she will try and
    keep the fondling of cylindrical objects nice and subtle,
    otherwise it could be a bit scary

Women also use preening techniques, smoothing clothes, touching hair, etc. A good 'come on' is a sexy walk across a room with the hips rolling to accentuate the pelvic region. Of course all this is meant to come naturally. Don't, whatever you do, think, 'Right now I'm going to do a sexy walk, rolling my hips to accentuate the pelvic region.' If you try too hard, you will look like you need a double hip replacement.

Women use eye make-up to emphasise their eyes. Fluttering eye lashes and come-to-bed eyes are a way of sending out signals. Masses of eyeshadow is also a way of marking your territory. Once you've smeared it all over his pillow cases you're saying, 'This is my patch – keep out bitches.'

Whether seated or standing in the company of a member of the opposite sex, both men and women have their legs open wider than normal. Women, be very careful of this wide-legged manoeuvre. When we say 'wider than normal', we don't mean gaping – you're not supposed to sit there like you're halfway through a Bob Fosse number.

If you are eyeing someone up, or they are doing this to you, look for the 'intimate gaze'. It falls across the eyes and below the chin to the triangular area between the chest and the crotch. Men and women use this gaze to show interest in each other, and those who are interested will return the gaze. (Information packs with plasticine available on request and a s.a.e.)

GETTING CRUSHES

Tragically, just because you are a Grumpy Old Man or Woman, it doesn't mean that you are immune to falling for people and having silly affairs, often – in fact invariably – with entirely inappropriate people. Crushes when you are over forty are a touch embarrassing, whereas if you are sixteen they are endearing or cute. When you are old enough to have someone ask if you are a concession at the cinema, you are too old to be having crushes. Which is not to say that you should be banned from some extracurricular sex, which I suppose might fall into the category of 'nice work if you can get it'.

Thing is, you can either 'go for it' and sit there flicking your hair with your legs wide open staring at his crotch and making masturbatory gestures on your wine glass, or pull yourself together and realise that the crush you have on your daughter's Latin teacher is a hopeless nonstarter.

Of course the kind of people you fancy as a grumpy are entirely different from the sort you had crushes on or fancied when you were young, or at least this applies to women. I find myself now fancying men who are basically a bit podgy, with thinning or greying hair, but with say a nice taste in shoes or reading specs. I like a practical man, or someone with a fierce sense of sharpness or wit. For instance, when I watch *The Apprentice* I find myself fancying that bloke who sits on Alan Sugar's left, even though he looks like a headmaster and he certainly isn't a sex god, which is nature's way of ensuring, I suppose, the minimum of disappointment for women of my age. I mean it would be no good going for someone like Simon Cowell would it, even if I wanted to. He would be surrounded by thousands of younger women who want his power and money.

I never ever thought I'd ever fancy a man who wore a tie with a matching pocket handkerchief – but there's this Channel 4 newsreader ... Jon Snow – swoon.   JENNY ECLAIR

This brings us to the tragic mismatch between male and female grumpies. Men who are that bit older still harbour a desire for the younger, slimmer, less wrinkly woman, and maddeningly they often seem to manage to get one. If they're successful, if they're wealthy, and they still have their own teeth, frankly ... if they want some, they can go and get some nooky with younger women. This is partly, I assume, because there are many more women on the market who are over forty than there are men, but also men are far more delusional when it comes to their ongoing sexual attraction.

Age gaps seem like a good idea at the time, but believe me the appeal wears off. OK, so she might be a babe compared to your ex-wife, but she won't know the same songs as you and she won't know what you're talking about when you refer to John Noakes or Radio Caroline.

Mind you, why is it that women kid themselves that this common-ground stuff is important? We're deluding ourselves! Given the choice between a) chuckling away on the sofa with a woman the same age, perhaps reminiscing about Bleep and Booster or b) having ice cubes rubbed over their nipples by a 19-year-old exotic dancer ... Hmmm, which way do you think the pendulum would swing?

Please don't bother sending your response on a postcard; we can guess the answer.

Here are some men renowned for their success with younger women:

Jack Nicholson
Rod Stewart
Peter Stringfellow
Hugh Hefner
Andrew Lloyd Webber
Mick Jagger
Michael Douglas
Simon Cowell

On the other hand here are some lucky girls who seem to bag more than their share of younger men:

Joan Collins
Demi Moore
Zsa Zsa Gabor

Barbara Windsor
Sadie Frost
Madonna
Liza Minnelli
Susan Sarandon
Eva Longoria
Samantha in *Sex and the City*

INTERNET DATING

These days dating is big business. Everyone is too busy with their BlackBerries to wait until they bump into someone who they fancy enough to go out with, so people go speed dating, or speed shagging, or answer ads or join expensive dating clubs, or indeed they use the internet. This is fine as long as you remember that everyone, but everyone lies when they post their details on the internet or in a personal ad. People fib in the way they do on their c.v. or in a job interview. So as long as you bear this in mind you can be fore-warned, but it's important that you can decode some of the key descriptions to avoid disappointment further down the line (when you meet them). Remember, when you are dating someone on the internet you don't know – literally – where they've been.

Fun loving is code for likes frolics in bed, probably threesomes

Young looking means well over preferred age range

Young at heart is likely to indicate someone eligible for a
    pension

GSOH means you have no sense of humour whatsoever, since
    anyone who puts that can't think of an amusing or original
    way of saying it

Slim means going to WeightWatchers

Tall means wears stack heels

Would like to meet the man of her dreams = emotionally
    dysfunctional

Would like to meet the woman of his dreams = mummy's boy
High earner = on commission – probably a sales rep
Financially independent – just been through hideous divorce

Even photographs can be misleading, in fact they will definitely be misleading. Some of them will bear no resemblance at all to the person you might meet in the flesh. No – in some ways meeting potential dates by accident or in real life has a lot going for it.

PLACES TO PULL

If, God forbid, you do find yourself back in the dating game at an advanced age, then frankly it is going to be very hard work indeed. You are going to have to join evening classes or choirs or dinner date evenings, so you might as well lower your standards drastically and go for the (even) older woman or man because let's face it the much older woman or man is almost certainly going to be grateful. Someone grateful is a wonderful thing, especially if they're so grateful that when they die they leave you all their worldly goods – thereby making you a more attractive proposition to a younger man or woman. Before you know it you could be on your third marriage, you devil.

If you are an oldie and you are dating or trying to date, where on earth would you go to pick someone up? You can hardly go to a bar or a club; you'd stick out like a weirdly dressed sore thumb. No, you need to go somewhere where you're going to blend in and be surrounded by like-minded folk. What about the early bird swim, or the local tip? And remember if all else fails, get a dog. You might meet someone in the park and if you don't, at least you've got a lovely smelly licky old dog.

TIPS FOR PULLING

Don't bat out of your league. For example, you might fancy George Clooney, but you're not going to get him, so you've got to go for the bloke who looks a bit like George Clooney's fat cousin who sells kebabs in Leicester Square, and maybe you'll be in with a chance.

Some more pulling tips ...

If you're really not sure, pretend to faint whilst you chat him up. If he uses it as an excuse to get the hell away, and treads on your leg as he trots off, then you have learnt a valuable if humiliating lesson. If he takes command, orders everyone to stand back, feels your pulse and orders you a brandy – he's worth digging your claws in as hard as possible

Of course there are some people who can't tell the difference between a girl fainting and a girl falling to the floor because she is drop-down drunk.

Don't drink too much, men might like you a little tiddly but they will become terrified if you start shouting at buses and trying to fight lamp posts. If you want a short sharp lesson in how women look really bad when they are drunk, treat yourself to a trip round Covent Garden or any city centre at midnight and you will see hordes of girls puking with their make-up round their ears – which is a bad look at twenty but at forty is disastrous.

Never drink so much that you are sick, then try and drink some more. This is a one-way ticket onto *The Jeremy Kyle Show*.

Smoking. The great thing about the smoking ban is that it's forced all the leftover smokers outside. This is great, as all the smokers now know who each other are and they can all get off with each other and swap stinky-breathed, nicotine-flavoured kisses amongst like-minded types. It is of course a myth that all the most interesting people are standing outside in the garden at parties smoking. This used to be true but now that Jenny has given up the fags it is no longer the case.

KISSING

Knowing whether someone wants to kiss you is critical with flirting, since kissing is the logical conclusion to flirting. Are they staring at you and giving you more eye contact than normal, are they standing closer than a friend or business colleague would? If so, this person probably wants to go for it. Alternatively, they might be about to punch or mug you. The trick is to be able to tell the difference. Wouldn't it be marvellous if every old woman who was about to be mugged had the foresight to snog her attacker before he struck? The resulting confusion would put paid to any purse swiping and be a genius solution to our criminal hoodie culture.

> *All kissing is a complete waste of time; I really don't see the point of it. I mean human beings haven't always kissed as a means of showing romance. When you examine it, it's a completely ridiculous thing to do.*   MATTHEW PARRIS

Kissing someone for the first time is very sexy indeed, and this is the bit of flirting that we oldies miss out on, as long as they don't do too much rummaging around in your mouth, trying to fish out bits of meat that you'd be better off trying to get out yourself later – this is emphatically over-enthusiastic kissing. No, less is definitely more with kissing, and kissing when it works is very, very good, if only because you can do it into old age when your fanny has well and truly dried up. But leave it too long and you'll be too old to kiss someone new as your teeth might ping out at the last minute – and kissing without your teeth in might be a bit of an acquired taste.

If the flirting and kissing works, then the chances are it's going to lead to some sex with someone for the first time, which is perhaps something that hasn't happened to you for several decades. It will almost certainly mean that you will want the room to be very dark indeed, since – unless you have prepared for it – you will be wearing hideous underwear and will have to hold in a bit of middle-aged spread.

> *I have this rule that I will not kiss a man on the lips unless I mean to go to bed with him.*   GERMAINE GREER

SEX WITH SOMEONE FOR THE FIRST TIME

You had forgotten how awkward it is, like a badly choreographed dance, because your Grumpy Old Partner and you had worked it all out, the docking procedure was seamless if dull, and you knew what each of you like. Get a new lover and you have to start from scratch, which I guess might be kind of fun, but it also might be rather tiring and take a long time, when really we would rather be getting on with some little jobs or putting some clean washing away in the airing cupboard.

Fact. Four out of ten women recently surveyed said they'd rather be browsing in John Lewis than getting jiggy between the sheets. We just made that up, but we bet it's true … especially round ladies separates.

Dressing for sex

Take off your dressing gown, and take out the gum guard that the dentist has given you to stop you grinding your teeth or prevent you from snoring. In our house there is an his and hers dental appliance next to the bed. He has one that makes him look like Hannibal Lecter and I have one that makes me look like a rugby player who has let himself go or a boxer with frizzy hair.

As a rule, ninety-nine times out of a hundred, it's better the devil you know. OK, so the old man might leave his toe-nail clippings on the edge of the bath, he might do that thing of forgetting you are self-conscious about your wobbly tummy and knead it like a big wad of dough, he might bring a tub of Häagen-Dazs to bed and forget to do anything more imaginative than eat the whole bloody lot himself – really slowly with a teaspoon so that he's still slurping after midnight. The one thing you don't have to worry about once you're a certain age and you've been together for a billion years is condoms.

Imagine going through all that fumbling again, imagine having to put your varifocals on to check the sell-by date, imagine he'd bought some pineapple- and mandarin-flavoured glow-in-the-dark ones – imagine ... Oh please, no more imagining, it's making us feel queasy.

The one big advantage of being a Grumpy Old Couple is that with any luck, and as long as your partner doesn't run off with the chiropodist or log on to Friends Reunited and look up an old flame (VERY DANGEROUS) you can be spared flirting for the foreseeable future. You do not need to bag another partner or get off with someone, or cop off to use that vile phrase. You can relax.

If a couple kiss for as little as twenty seconds a day it would improve their relationship. Twenty seconds, that's all it takes, but kissing is the first thing to go when things go wrong.   TRACEY COX

3 · Courting or becoming a couple in the first place

As we pointed out in the previous chapter most of us decide who we fancy instantly, instinctively and spontaneously. Grumpy Old Matthew Parris says you can check this theory out by getting stuck at Amsterdam Airport with three hours to kill; just sit and watch people walk by and decide in a flash whether you fancy them or not, or whether – at a pinch – you'd sleep with them.

It is truly astonishing how quickly and decisively you can put people into one camp or the other. It's fun to compare notes and see what percentage of people who walk past fall into the 'would sleep with at a pinch' or 'no not never' category. Fun, but it probably doesn't make up for being stuck at Amsterdam Airport – unless of course by some weird freak of fate you happen to meet the love of your life there (or someone you can't resist having a knee tremble with in a mop cupboard).

Whatever. We know that whoever we eventually set up house with was originally assessed as soon as we set eyes on them. On that very first meeting we sussed out the essentials, such as shoes, bra size, dental hygiene, etc., and hey presto the rest eventually was history.

FIRST IMPRESSIONS THAT MIGHT INFLUENCE YOUR JUDGEMENT

He is getting out of a Porsche or stepping off his own private
    yacht/jet

She is riding a bicycle; there are flowers and a stick of French
    bread in the basket hanging from the handlebars

He has just saved a small child from drowning

He has hair on his head and all his own teeth

She is wearing a small bikini and laughing

He is in a fireman's uniform, a real one and he is on a fire
    engine going to an emergency

He is walking an Airedale (sorry but have a thing about
    Airedales – J.E.)

She has just won the Lottery

She is walking her frail old dad round the park on a Sunday

He hands you his half-used pay and display ticket and asks if
    you'd like it

He has had his hair permed or coloured

She is wearing white shoes

He is wearing white shoes

She has a big bad dog with a jewel-encrusted collar that is so bad
    that it has to have a toddler-type rein as a lead

He hangs about in multi-storey car parks

A development of the airport game is the shag, marry or chuck off
a cliff game. Basically someone throws you the name of someone
of the opposite sex; it can be a celebrity, someone you know, or
indeed the person sitting next to you, and you have to decide what
you would rather do with them: shag, marry or chuck off a mountain.

This can get hurtful, especially if friends include you – and
you are not drunk enough to think that it's remotely funny that
the friend (that you actually fancy a bit) would rather chuck you
off a cliff than shag you.

Jenny's list

Here is a list of people that, if forced, Jenny would shag:

Jude Law
That technician at the theatre in Crawley
Christopher Walken
Shane Ritchie – yes, I don't care
James McAvoy
Gordon Ramsay
Judith's husband

Here is a list of people Jenny would marry:

Martin Clunes
Michael Palin
That nice Bill Turnbull who reads the news on the BBC

Here's a list of people Jenny would rather chuck off a cliff:

Louis Walsh
Craig Revel Horwood
Jimmy Saville

Judith's list

If forced Judith would shag:

Anyone with their own private jet (with the exception of Simon
    Cowell, Michael Jackson or Peter Stringfellow) ... but we
    would have to be on our way to his own private Caribbean
    island and even then I would insist on my own room

Here is a list of people Judith would marry:

Jenny's partner – serves her right for putting my husband on
    her shag list
Steve Martin

Jeremy Paxman
Laurence Llewelyn-Bowen – I know it's weird
Stuart Maconie – makes me laugh so much
Jonathan Ross but floppy hair would have to be pinned back
    with either Kirby grips or a hairband

Judith would rather chuck off a cliff:

Bill Oddie
John Noakes
John Humphrys
Prince Andrew – he's a waste of food, and quite a lot of it
Richard Hammond – I am about twice his size (not sexy for a
    woman and a bit weird for the bloke)
Rolf Harris
George Clooney – too much competition from other women
    and must have an ego the size of a planet
Nigel Havers – would make me feel too working-class
Richard Branson
Andrew Neil
Michael Portillo

As you can see Judith is a lot more picky than Jenny.

LUST OR LOVE AT FIRST SIGHT

*I do totally believe in love at first sight. I fell in love with my
husband at first sight and it lasted for thirty-odd years until he
died.* LYNN BARBER

*I believe enormously in love at first sight. I think if it doesn't go
ping inside sixty seconds the chances of it happening after that are
pretty slight.* STEVEN NORRIS

How can you possibly fall in love at first sight? Utter rubbish.
But yes, you can be completely overcome with rampaging lust at
first sight.   KATHRYN FLETT

When you decide you fancy someone, and the mood takes you, it is invariably one of two things that sparks things off ... either lust or love. Lust is the kind of sexual chemistry that means you want to get their kit off urgently, and love is the kind of chemistry that means you are likely to be lying on your back looking at the stars and feeling you have found your soulmate. Both states or stages are likely of course to include alcohol – and so most of the time they can't be taken seriously or as a sign that this person is a potential life partner. However, getting the two things – lust and love at first sight together – is a very wonderful, and very rare, phenomenon and this is when the trouble starts, because you are drawn to becoming a proper couple with the same answer machine and electricity bill. So savour the memory of that first really magical bit, because we are here to tell you, as if you didn't already know, that this will not last.

Lust is biological. The sex hormones testosterone and oestrogen in both men and women do weird things to our brain (and other bits); they literally light up parts of the brain that you can see on an MRI scan – although it might break up the moment somewhat if you did – and the hormones are linked to the same reward system that can cause drug addiction. Lust, therefore, is officially addictive.

To put it into perspective though, other addictive substances include:

Chocolate
Heroin
Sausages (cold) dipped in a really good mustard
Nicotine
Alcohol
Collecting china owls

Even animals do a bit of falling in love apparently. They display signs of courtship – stroking, licking and caressing – but let's not go there; it can only lead to talk of dogs and bottom sniffing. Attraction generally lasts seconds in rats, three days among elephants and months in dogs. For some reason human beings are supposed to find one another attractive for twenty or thirty years. No wonder we hit problems.

The swan, however, is the most naturally monogamous amongst all of us. Once they find a mate, that's it. No more necking other swans in the bulrushes.

Of course this sort of single-mindedness can backfire. There was a true story some time ago about a swan who fell in love with a swan-shaped paddle boat and had to be removed to a zoo for her own sanity.

Swans are in fact the only non-human species whose behaviour is like ours in terms of love, mates and children. If a mate is lost they go through a grieving process before flying off to find a new stretch of water to live on where they may find a new mate. Swans live with their mum and dad till they are four (probably about eighteen in human years – unless they are doing a gap year), then they leave home and look for a mate of their own. If the cygnets stay any longer than that, the parents can turn nasty and cut parental ties by chasing the little ones away. In human terms this would coincide with the human parents pulling themselves together about blubbing about their little darlings leaving home and realising that they like coming back to a tidy house at the end of the day and realising how much money they save on the immersion heater. Then the cygnets have to join the first flock of swans they encounter, where they can live till they mature and find a mate themselves.

LOVE AND LUST

Here are some examples of how these things can take hold ... based on true life as experienced by Jenny Eclair and Judith Holder:

When I – Jenny Eclair – was twelve I fell in lust with Paul Newman. I knew something was going on when I felt the urge to peel off my socks whilst I was watching one of his movies. Had it not been a Sunday night in front of the telly with the family I might have been tempted to have gone further. This was my first experience of sexual stirring, other than climbing the rope during school gym lessons.

Ten years later I was working in a café in Covent Garden and I saw a man sitting at table five. I said to my friend Philippa, 'He's mine, the man at table five is mine, I love him and I'm going to have his children.'

Twenty-five years on, Geof and I have a daughter and are still together. 'He's the only thing I have ever been sure about.'

Between Paul Newman and St Geof (as all my friends and family call him) there have been numerous snogs, shags and near misses. Even now there will be the occasional glance that gets me hot under the collar, and I look at lovely young men on the street all the time and I think, 'How pretty you are.' In fact, recently in Edinburgh there was a couple in their late teens/early twenties and they were so gorgeous and in love that I had a bit of a cry. That said, I saw a really old couple holding hands on the bus and that made me cry too – God I'm getting soft.

When Judith was sixteen she lusted after her English teacher called Mr Cobb because he was really cool. He introduced himself as David Cobb (first names!!) and at that moment Judith decided she was going to get really good at English and stay behind and do S-level English and babysit for his children. Unfortunately he had a very pretty wife, but the good news is Judith got fabulous English grades and went to university to read English, not because she liked reading (at all) but because she liked David Cobb. Judith would rather write essays on Milton than try to flirt with someone, but secretly she always hopes it will have the same effect.

Judith lusted after someone at university who ran the TV student network thing, which sounds grander than it really was. He was all bossy and clever and studious and Judith being the ambitious cow that she is went all weak at the knees when he came in the room and offered to floor manage and do all the dreary things that he didn't want to do. He became a famous TV reporter and Judith became a TV producer, but as usual Judith didn't dare utter a word, or dare even a teeny bit of flirting. Judith later had a serious crush on someone at work, and instead of asking him out she went football training with him every Wednesday night, and instead of him realising that she fancied him, he just thought she liked football. Durr. How hopeless she was/is. What a good thing she no longer has to flirt with anyone.

Although lust is a very powerful thing, the fact is, love is more powerful than lust. That's why people cry at big soppy romantic movies like *Titanic* and *Gone with the Wind* and not at one of those 'confessions of a window cleaner' films.

LUST BEWARE

Lust is one of the seven deadly sins; love is patient, love is kind (according to the Bible, some of us would say this is pushing it a bit)

Lust is what can get people into trouble, it is lust that makes couples have sex in lifts; love is what makes people go out and choose carpets together

Lust is what makes women cop off with a 'grubby scaffolder'; love is what happens when the 'grubby scaffolder' turns out to own the apartment block

COURTING

In the olden days, before Sky+, going out with someone was called 'courting'. When girls tried to keep a bit of mystery and spent their whole time scrutinising the Cathy and Claire problem page in *Jackie* magazine for clues as to how to snog a boy, and when meeting potential snogees happened over lashings of ping pong at the youth club.

These days 'mystery' is a thing of the past, unless you're a Christian, or Muslim, and 'courting' or 'going out' is dispensed with entirely in favour of casual sex – by which we don't mean having sex in a second-best cardigan.

Now you don't flirt, you 'hit on someone', which seems an odd phrase, and these days people are 'hot' – not fanciable or dishy (very dating) – or they're 'fit', which doesn't mean they do circuit training on Wednesday nights, but that they're hot stuff. Why can't people just leave things as they are – all this changing of words and phrases and street speak leads to making us grumpies look like old fogies and our children assuming that we know nothing about sex or drugs and rock 'n' roll at all.

The whole business of dating and getting off with someone, and girlfriends and boyfriends, has gone a bit off-message as far as we grumpies are concerned. Young people, as we like to call them, seem to jump into bed with one another for no reason whatsoever. Shagging or bonking, as we used to call it, seems to happen at the drop of a hat; it is no big deal (not unless you catch chlamydia of course, in which case it is a very big deal indeed). How would they like it if we oldies started to behave like this, if we started flaunting our sex drive in public, getting down and dirty on a park bench or rubbing ourselves up and down on our shopping trolleys or doing some heavy petting in a parked car?

In fact I think some like-minded grumpy vigilantes should group together and, in a bid to put a stop to all this public display of teenage sexuality, we should play them at their own game. Yes,

large groups of oldies should gather where the young ones gather – in shopping malls and outside chip shops – and have a mass group slobber. Loads of us snogging and groping each other – see how the youngsters would like that? They wouldn't, oh no, they'd run home screaming. Good. A simple and cheap method of ridding our streets of hoodie scum; more effective than an asbo. Hoorah, grumpies win again.

CHAT-UP LINES

Chat ups are very, very tricky indeed. You can flirt and pout and glare and tease visually – and if you do it right it can be very effective – but once you open your mouth and say something you are committing yourself somewhat. A bad chat up and there is no way back.

Professor Richard Wiseman has done some serious research about chat-up lines, and has concluded that a good chat-up line is an open question – like, 'What do you like doing in your spare time?' In other words you can't answer 'Yes' or 'No'. So, for instance, 'Do you come here often?' is a no-no because he or she can just say 'Yes' or 'No', whereas something that means they have to give something away is a good thing. Which all seems very sensible except that he also concluded that the best chat-up line – the most effective one – is, 'What sort of pizza topping do you like the best?' Which frankly would send me running in the opposite direction but each to his or her own.

Some bad chat up lines:

I'm a bit drunk, and I'm finding you very attractive

Translation: however, if I was stone cold sober, I wouldn't go anywhere near you, you freak of nature

Shall I bring the etchings down to you?

Translation: I am an idiot

If you were an animal what would you be?

Translation: because I am slimy and a bit creepy, therefore I would be a slug

Chat-up lines are never as good as just plain begging.
LAURENCE LLEWELYN-BOWEN

*It doesn't matter if it's corny. If they like you, they'll forgive you.
It's just about opening up and being honest and just saying,
'Look, I'm really nervous but I've been watching you across
the bar and you're very attractive, and can I have a shag?'*
BRIAN CONLEY

*I've probably said, 'I do find Dylan Thomas's later work very
apocalyptic, don't you?' which basically means can I have a shag,
but it's just dressed up better, isn't it?*   STUART MACONIE

*Because of the way I am, people have probably just gone,
'Are you on for a shag?'*   ARABELLA WEIR

The biggest problem of course for the middle-aged grumpy out
on the pull is actually hearing the chat-up line. If, God help you,
you're in a noisy club or a busy bar, the chances of actually catching
what he's said are virtually nil.

Poor thing, just imagine he's spent hours plucking up the
courage to deliver his best chat-up line as close to your ear as
possible and all you do is yell, 'Eh ... what, sorry, beg your pardon?'
back in his face.

Frankly chat-up lines just make you look a bit sad and desperate, and desperate signals as we all know are the biggest turn off
of all.

As we all know actions speak louder. If he throws popcorn at
you, he fancies you – 'twas ever thus.

Seriously blokes, forget the cheesy chat-up lines; do something
useful instead. Go round to her house and re-grout her bathroom.
She might be so grateful and fancy you so much that you end up in
the shower together having lots of rude sex. Who knows? It's worth
a try.

Women. If you fancy him, undo that button on your blouse and buy him a pork pie. If he's still not interested, give up.

Actually, lots of courting rituals are easier now than they were back in the seventies when a lot of us grumpies were teenagers. For example, downloading a compilation of songs from your iTunes and burning them onto a CD is a piece of cake compared to all that pausing and pressing play on your tape recorder. Cor what a palaver that used to be, as messy and time-consuming as giving love-bites, which is something else we don't need to bother about any more.

Is there anything so grim as the sight of a hickey on a fiftysomething? Erghhhhhhhh.

In fact, technology in general makes the whole thing both harder and easier. In the old days if you didn't want to talk to a boy on the phone, you'd get your mum to tell him you weren't in. Nowadays, thanks to mobile phones, when he leaves you a message asking you out on a date you can just text 'am washing hair' and he'll get the message quick enough.

WHAT TO LOOK FOR IN A POTENTIAL MATE

The problem with being a Grumpy Old Couple is that the qualities that you looked for in a partner when you were in your twenties and thirties are now irrelevant. Their love of the Moody Blues and their curly blonde hair are long since gone ... and have been replaced by an obsession with filing their vinyl collection alphabetically or an overly diligent amount of attention paid to their bowel movements. When I was young I wanted someone who looked like Ilia Kuriakin, had a full head of hair and a pair of loons. Now standards have dropped. If I were in the dating game, which thank goodness I am not, I would go for someone who had their own teeth and knew how to use a power drill.

No. Much better to go for the things that last: i.e. money and a sense of humour.

Money

Some people say that money is irrelevant when it comes to relationships, but they're being economical with the truth. OK, so we'd all draw the line at Donald Trump (well most of us would surely to goodness), but on the whole – be honest – money is attractive in a potential partner/spouse/mate.

However, money can be a turn-off when it's exhibited in the wrong way – for example:

Showy-offy open-top sports cars. OK if you are over eighteen (otherwise daddy bought it) or under fifty (otherwise your pension payout bought it). And it's not OK to wear a silly hat. Deer-stalking hats are an especially bad sign.

Designer handbags and bling in a woman. She is not going to be willing to rinse out the swing bin or notice when bin liners need buying. She will want a lot of pamper days and expensive birthday presents (jewellery probably), and she won't put any petrol in the car. Trust us, this sort of woman is going to be high maintenance.

Complicated legal arrangements with ex-wives or girlfriends. They will want you to sign a prenuptial agreement and in any case the more ex-wives there are, the more swimming pools and billiard rooms there are to maintain.

Otherwise money is a good thing. Why? Here are things that money can buy:

Lunch at the Wolseley
Tickets to see a nice musical plus gin and tonics in the interval
The occasional cab rather than a night bus
Your sinuses drained privately rather than waiting for three years on the NHS
Romantic weekend breaks
Organic broccoli
Decent dental work

Some properly scientific people have done research on this topic of money would you believe. One university asked 30,000 men from 170 countries a bunch of questions about their sex lives, and guess what they found out ... that the more money a man makes, the more sex he has. Gasp and then gasp again, and the more money he makes, the more opportunity he has to have sex with a wider variety of partners. Conversely, the more broke a man is financially the less sex he has and the fewer women he has a chance to shag. Well well ... And someone probably spent a lot of time doing that research. Frankly we could have told them that for free.

And there we were thinking that women were after nice genes for their children. No, women are just pragmatic: they like nice things and nice hairdos, and nice holidays, and they want someone to come in to clean the kitchen floor for them. End of story.

However, does it work the other way? Do women entrepreneurs or women with a lot of money from Mummy and Daddy benefit from interest in the opposite sex in the same way?

Apparently not. Women do not seem to benefit one bit from having money in the sex stakes. Becoming a stakeholder or hedge-fund manager can only end in tears as far as women go on the sex front. Men are apparently scared of women with money. And guess what? Men are still primarily concerned above all else with ... a woman's looks, which is depressing when you're turning into Camilla Parker Bowles.

Even women don't like powerful women that much.

Madonna is possibly the most successful recording artist of her generation but women secretly think she's looking a bit scraggy round the neck, and the video when she was pushing her 50-odd-year-old purple-lycra-clad pudenda into the camera was ... 'a bit much'.

Most men, on the other hand, are just really scared of her.

The thing is, men know that Madonna wouldn't be very sympathetic if you pulled your back trying to find the free Winnie the Pooh DVD that fell out of the Saturday *Express* and disappeared behind the sofa.

Humour

A sense of humour is important in a relationship, and the older and grumpier a couple get the more crucial the sense of humour is. How else will you (both) get through the menopause? The things that make you laugh will change with time, obviously. You used to laugh at his cute way of making cocktails, he used to laugh at your girly hopeless way of parallel parking, but twenty years on both of these things just annoy the hell out of you, so you will have to move on to other things to laugh at – hopefully.

There's nothing worse though than someone who thinks they are crazily, fabulously funny who is really not. Anyone who has to work hard at telling the world that they are funny is to be taken with a huge pinch of salt. People who put ads in lonely-hearts columns and say they have a GSOH almost invariably mean they like reruns of the Goodies or the Goons or have a funny hat with a hammer on, or they have crazy friends or crazy wild wacky times on holiday. Date these people with caution; they are actually very dreary indeed. Some people just don't have any idea where to draw the 'funny' line. The last thing you want is someone who is going to find it funny when you fall down a manhole in Karachi or someone who is going to watch you slip on some turkey fat on Christmas Day and fall over with laughter, or someone who knows where you hide your chocolate and moves it just when you most want it. You don't want someone who tickles you, which when you are over forty is probably physically dangerous. You certainly don't want anyone who tells jokes. Jokes are to women what embroidery is to men. They don't get it, and don't want to get it. Which is why women can never remember the punch lines to jokes, or even the bit leading up to the punch lines. They never know when to laugh, so they laugh in the wrong place and the person telling the joke has to start the joke again and the whole thing is just agony. No, women hate jokes almost as much as they hate chat-up lines. Both are equally off-putting.

My partner only really laughs at me when I have fallen over or hurt myself. Once I tripped over a rabbit hole in Cornwall and he was in fits. I have a horrible feeling that if I die of a massive heart attack, my last living memory as I clutch my chest and stagger round the sitting room will be of him chortling away in the corner. JENNY ECLAIR

Eric Bressler, a graduate student at McMaster University, who is studying the role of humour in personal attraction, discovered in a survey of 150 students that to a woman a sense of humour means someone who makes her laugh, but to a man a sense of humour means someone who appreciates his jokes. No wonder the divorce rate is so high.

Women laugh at men's jokes, not only out of politeness but in the knowledge that it makes their breasts jiggle a little, something a man finds just as attractive as the fact that she laughs at his crap jokes – ah, who is the clever one here?

Voices as a turn-on

Voices are an important part of someone's attractiveness. Women are especially partial to men with low voices, according to research. So they like a man who talks well, and they like a man with a deep voice. The proof of this particular pudding was the thrice-married Barry White who, despite being the size of a small block of flats, had a real way with the ladies.

In a survey Wayne Rooney topped the poll in the list for the least sexy male accent with 78% of the female vote. 61% of ladies liked a deep and husky voice, whereas David Beckham's high-pitched voice was seen as a turn-off.

58% of men surveyed also liked smouldering and smokey voices in a woman, as with DJ Emma B.

Posh voices are not popular: only 12% of females and 9% of men questioned liked them, though a posh gravelly voice, á la Joanna Lumley, gets a thumbs up from the boys.

Accents also play a part in the courting ritual, apparently ... According to a survey for Speed Dating London:

The top 5 accents men go for are:

Essex (41%)
Welsh (38%)
Scottish (12%)
West Country (8%)
Birmingham (5%)

Hmm. Essex accents win?! All down to the voice and nothing to do with their reputation as goers? Hmmmm. Whereas the ladies like:

Scottish (35%)
Birmingham (16%)
Mancunian (18%)
Scouse (17%)
Welsh (5%)

Again, has this really got anything to do with accents? Is it not more to do with the kilt factor?

Already there is a nasty pattern of discrepancy in terms of what both sexes want. No wonder things go horribly wrong on the dating scene.

More internationally, Australians have the sauciest accents. According to one in five women, and nearly a quarter of men, they like the Italian accent best of all – but then again we are told they are fabulous lovers. WHO SAYS? THEY DO! Source: Mates Survey.

AS A WOMAN GETS OLDER, SHE GETS CHOOSIER

When you are young you don't mind if your latest bloke can't actually do anything but roll the occasional joint, but as one wises up the incompetent male becomes less and less attractive.

Here is a tick list of things a man should be able to do. If he can't do more than three of these things, don't say you haven't been warned:

Drive
Ride a bike
Swim
Withstand very cold temperatures so that you can borrow his
    coat (he mustn't shiver – that's very unattractive)
Whittle a stick
Catch a ball
Not be scared of dogs, so much so that he has to walk the long
    way round because there's a barking Alsatian on the corner
Make toast

THINGS THAT MIGHT PUT A WOMAN OFF A GRUMPY OLD MAN

White socks, black shoes

A packed lunch eater

A man reading a daft book like *The Da Vinci Code*. Here's the ultimate turn-off: a man wearing white socks with black shoes, eating a packed lunch while reading *The Da Vinci Code* and then to top it all off he picks his nose, cleans a bit of wax out of his ear and then sniffs it

Anyone who has traced their family tree

THINGS THAT MIGHT PUT A BLOKE OFF A GRUMPY OLD WOMAN

Control issues – why is it so hard to delegate anything

Who cares whether the dishcloth is clean, it's just a dishcloth

It's one rule for her and another rule for everyone else; for some reason she goes ballistic when someone leaves the immersion on and then when she leaves it on for a weekend she says she was too busy to turn it off

She borrows your razor to shave her chin – not just her underarms

She borrows your nasal hair tweezers

She snores, but complains about everyone else snoring

She complains full stop

Her mess is OK, everyone else's is a big, big drama

She lets herself go and then complains when she looks fat

She asks you if she looks fat and then you tell her she does and she thinks it's your fault

Despite there being many reasons for a man and a woman not to get together, they do and once they are serious about their intentions towards each other (i.e. no more snogging other people) there are lots of traditions that need to be undertaken – not least getting to know each other's friends and family.

MEETING THE PARENTS RULES FOR HIM

Do

Eat nicely with a knife and fork (in the correct hands)

Obviously that's only if you are having a meal, don't just demonstrate your knife and fork skills for the sake of it; they will think you are weird

Say please and thank you

Be nice to the dog, even if it's a really horrible dog

Feign interest in her dad's koi carp. However, do put down some firm boundaries. Be interested, but don't pretend you are really, really interested, or he will get you to subscribe to some very dodgy magazines

Compliment her mother on the house, her cooking or her garden, but not her figure, otherwise she will think you are a sex pest

Don't

Sit in her dad's chair

Light your own fart – not even after the meal

Talk about your overdraft – even if you say afterwards you were only kidding, they will remain suspicious

Ask them about their financial assets – or if you do be subtle about it

Say anything even remotely critical about their daughter. This could lead to her father running you over accidentally on purpose when you help him open the garage door next day

MEETING THE PARENTS RULES FOR HER

Do

Pretend to be nicer than you are

Offer to help stack the dishwasher. However, don't get carried away. Don't bleach her dishcloths and start wiping down the skirting boards, or she will think you are 'dissing' her housekeeping

Pretend to like the same television programmes; don't say, '*Doc Martin*: what a load of crap'

Play up your liking of children and animals – it will stand you in good stead and they will think you are fragrant and kind

Don't

Show your tatoos

Don't say, 'Hmm, this is quite nice but when I make this I find adding a bit of chilli gives it some flavour'

Don't scratch your bottom, not even if it's really itchy

Don't criticise their son in any shape or form – it can only lead to a lifetime of revenge from your potential mother-in-law and believe me that could be very very scary indeed

Flirt with his father; not when SHE is looking anyway

Before you make any lifelong commitment to each other, it's important to remember that families aren't just for Xmas; they're for every other Sunday for lunch, birthdays, christenings and 'just popping in' if you're really unlucky. Do not join a family if:

They have an aquarium in the living room
They don't wipe their feet when they come in from the garden; you will not be able to train your future spouse to do so
They run fair rides
They have servants; you will be one too
They like kettle snacks and by kettle snacks we don't mean those rather superior hand-cooked crisps, we're talking meals that require only the pouring of hot water and can be eaten with a spoon

OTHER PEOPLE'S FAMILIES – WHAT TO WATCH OUT FOR

Women and their mothers

It is a well-known fact that women turn into their mothers. We're not saying men have to fancy their mothers-in-law, that would be wrong, but they should be able to stand being in the same room as them without grinding all the enamel off their teeth. If you can't, then your future looks rocky.

Beware

Women who have mothers who still buy their clothes, or who make their own Christmas decorations are a potential problem because they have so much time on their hands they will interfere with your lives, and once you have kids they will be impossible but make it look like they are being very generous. Women who have mothers who dominate their husbands are also something to look out for and are a danger signal. Their domination can manifest itself in many ways: their husbands have a long list of little jobs or errands to do constantly, they spend a lot of time in their sheds (in winter) and they wear their trousers high-waisted. The only thing you can do to counteract this is to take sides, gang up with the father-in-law, and encourage him to make home brew in the shed. When you visit, join him in the shed, and soon you'll have your own deckchair in there. Good. The witches can stay indoors and watch *Deal or No Deal*.

> *My partner wanted us to do a wife swap. He wanted to swap me for a shed.*   JENNY ECLAIR

Daughters and father figures

Any woman who calls her father Daddy should ring alarm bells. Daddy will always know best and know what to do in any situation and Daddy – naturally – is never going to like you.

The trouble with women who adored their father, and this of course is most of us, is that Daddy is an impossibly hard act to follow. Choose a husband who is totally polemically unlike your father to avoid comparisons and you will be forever wishing that your husband was as besotted as your dad was and be annoyed that he forgets to get the car serviced. Or alternatively marry someone who is on some level rather like your dad and you will forever be wishing you had married someone who set your loins on fire rather than one that could put some shelves up for you. Either way you are doomed.

> *My dad always has a red and white spotted hankie, my partner always has a red and white spotted hankie. Freudian or what?*
> JENNY ECLAIR

Women and their friends and their friends' children

Women who pretend they like people when they don't are danger-ous as a potential life partner ... in other words they have a family round for Sunday lunch, are charm itself, nothing is too much trouble, and then the moment their car pulls out of the drive they take everyone else in the family by surprise by saying, 'My God I thought they would never go' – and run up the stairs two at time to check whether the toddler has done a poo and not flushed it properly. They are two-faced cows. In other words, these women are very tricky to deal with. But then again this covers every woman we know so men you are a bit sunk to be honest.

Women and their children

What men sort of know, but try to ignore, is that once babies start arriving they slide down the scale of importance. Most women have never experienced love like the love that they have for their children, that ghastly all-encompassing obsessive love that turns women into rabid lionesses. Yes, we might love Daddy but if Daddy falls over in the sand pit, Mummy isn't going to give the bully who pushed him a 'taste of his own medicine'. Mummy might worry about Daddy driving on the motorway late at night but she's not likely to ring the police if he's more than three minutes late and Mummy is unlikely to stalk Daddy on the dangerous walk home from work to make sure he uses the zebra crossing. If Mummy did stuff like that she'd be mad. Ah, but these are all things we have done for our children. Fact: husbands are replaceable, children are not.

However, children do leave home eventually and it's important for empty nest grumpies to be able to pull themselves through this together. Why not find something you both enjoy doing? You might remember that sex was quite good. If not, try a jigsaw puzzle; just don't start drinking during the day.

Women and their sisters

Identical hairdos are a bad sign.

Women will be viciously critical of their sisters but woe betide you if you join in; it will backfire spectacularly. The other worry with sisters is the oldest one will always think the youngest one is the prettiest. God help you if you agree.

Remember you are in a no-win situation with sisters. They are a law unto themselves. Of course, if your sisters-in-law have all gone and married idiots, this is something that you and your wife are allowed to agree on and enjoy bitching about.

Men and their sisters

Men's sisters fall into two categories: know-it-all superior cows and needy-weepy basket cases.

Really it's best to weed out men with sisters; it's almost worth turning down a proposal of marriage over the matter. For some reason a lot of blokes' sisters are raving beauties – which is precisely what you don't want in a bridesmaid.

Women and their brothers

Women usually adore their brothers, unless they haven't got over that punching each other in the face thing, which can make a civilised family meal quite difficult. Again, brothers fall into two categories: the all-rounder Oxford Blue with periwinkle eyes and rippling torso, and the junkie scumbag thief. Either way they are a nuisance and will make you feel uncool, suburban and fat.

Men and their brothers

Oh God, what a can of worms. The worst-case scenario is an all-boys litter with no civilising sisters around. The all-male sibling scenario becomes heinously competitive and family occasions will always end up with someone breaking a collar bone. The non-sporty brothers will compete academically. Unfortunately there will always be a runt in the family, which will be the one who wants to marry you.

Men and their mothers

He might be 6 foot 3 but to his mum he is eternally her little boy. She will hate you, even though she will pretend she doesn't, Deep down she still wants him to marry her friend Jean's middle girl –

'such a nice girl'. She would poison you if she had the guts, but in the meantime she just spends every bridge or bingo session – depending on socioeconomics – slagging you off.

Men and their fathers

One or other will be a disappointment: always has been, always will be. For your sake it's best if it's the dad that's the disappointment rather than the son. Disappointing dads can vary from ne'er-do-well layabouts to pathological bullies.

HOW TO TELL WHEN YOU'VE BECOME A COUPLE

When you first get together, neither of you has any idea how long it's going to last, but there comes a time in a relationship when it is no longer the case that you are 'just dating'; an invisible line gets crossed and all of a sudden it's serious, you are a couple!

How do you know when you are a couple?

When you don't have to ask him how many sugars. You
    know it's two but you only ever put one in because you
    don't want him getting fat and being an embarrassment
When he doesn't get up off the sofa when your mum walks in
    the room (this is because his flies are undone and he doesn't
    want to draw attention to the fact)
He's been to the pub with your dad – without you
You book a holiday together – this is the biggy. If you book your
    summer holiday in January then you might as well book the
    church while you're at it; you have decided this relationship
    has legs, because once he sees yours, if and when you do go
    on that holiday, he might change his mind!

What to do next?

In the olden days young men and women rushed into marriage because they couldn't get enough decent sex whilst they were still living with their parents.

Even those who regularly had sex before marriage had never 'done it' in a double bed. A survey back in 1970 * asked a hundred young couples why they had got married and 97% of them said it was because they wanted to 'do it' in a double bed. There is no data to say whether doing it in a double bed was slightly more disappointing than most of them had anticipated.

Nowadays there is no need to jump into marriage. Let's face it, moving in together and buying a nice big king-sized double bed from IKEA is a lot cheaper than a church wedding complete with twelve bridesmaids and a sit-down buffet for 240.

Sometimes the very idea of marriage is enough to drive one screaming for the hills. Sometimes it's best to cohabit – just move in with him – even if he hasn't actually asked you!

> *When I moved in with my partner I did it by stealth. It was like* The Great Escape *in reverse. He was very reticent; he always says it's like a one-night stand that's gone horribly wrong. Twenty-five years on and he's still offering to run me down the bus stop.*
> JENNY ECLAIR

Of course there's usually a bit of a lull between first date and moving in together and many couples fall by the wayside. Here are some common causes of a relationship taking a metaphorical early bath:

He is posh, you are common
You are posh, he is common
You like dogs, he likes cats
You like cats, he likes dogs

* Obviously this survey is completely trumped up, but is probably as accurate as most surveys

He likes reptiles
You like Barry Manilow
You are 23, he is 59
You are 59 and he is 23 !!!!!!!!!

AGE GAPS

Age gaps are fine until one of you gets old. Then suddenly the older man becomes – well – an old man, or the older woman becomes an old woman, and the younger partner is left rather high and dry, and probably earning for two unless you are very lucky. This is the drawback to marrying a father figure; they really do turn into your father and then you are married to a man who likes a routine, and insists on fish knives for chip-shop fish and chips, which is clearly ludicrous. And for the older of the two partners, they are destined for a life of trying desperately to keep up and failing.

Of course the advantage of this kind of relationship is that the much older one might die and you are likely to benefit from their will – so it's not all doom, gloom and bed pans. But of course not all relationships end happily ever after. In fact, most don't. However, 'death' is usually the last thing on the list of reasons to never see each other again.

BEING DUMPED OR DUMPING

Sooner or later in the dating game you are probably going to be dumped or do some dumping, and dumping as we all know hurts. Sometimes it's hard to spot that you are being dumped, and I for one have been dumped by someone and I simply wasn't getting it – and didn't want to get it – because sometimes the words coming out of someone's mouth are a code language. For instance, 'We're getting too serious' means, in a dumping context, that they want out: this minute, that night, not to ease things off or see one another less frequently, because the chances are they have met someone else anyhow. Getting too serious is code for 'Bog off; get over it.'

I think you should always be honest, but there are degrees of honesty. I don't want to be with you any more because I have decided I want to be with your sister might be a step too far in the honesty stakes. JENNI TRENT HUGHES

How to know when you are being dumped

They want to meet you early evening and have plans later on
They say they need some space
Can't we just be friends
I really like you as a friend
You're not in my plans
I find you very sweet but ...

They say ... It's not you it's me ... Yes, right.

As soon as any woman finds you sweet you know that sexually you are now a tea cosy. 'Let's be friends' is the worst possible thing you can say to a man. Saying, 'You're really sweet, can't we be friends?' is like head-butting and then kneeing you in the groin. GUY BROWNING

The phrase 'It's not you, it's me', that's rubbish, isn't it? You'd actually prefer it if somebody said, 'Actually it's you, it's not me, I'm great but I just don't like you.' JUSTIN MOORHOUSE

What they usually mean is: I found someone else. In fact I found someone else about a month ago and now my schedule is getting over-complicated.

The other golden rule on dumping or being dumped more specifically is that there is no point at all in trying to argue your way out of it. To argue that surely, yes, we have differences, but look at the lovely time we both had on holiday. Once you're being dumped you're being dumped.

JENNY ECLAIR Q AND A ON DUMPING AND BEING DUMPED

Q: Have you ever experienced unrequited love? If so, how did you get over it?
A: I was dumped before my A levels. I drank the contents of my parents' drinks cabinet and threw myself downstairs. This was pre-Princess Diana.

Q: Why is it all so intense first time around/when you're in your teens? Or did you sail through and play the field?
A: I was a bit of a slag. I'm afraid I got over relationships quite well as I learnt from an early age that I don't look good crying. Also I was always too hungry to mope.

JUDITH HOLDER Q AND A ON DUMPING AND BEING DUMPED

Q: Were you usually the one doing the dumping or usually the one being dumped?
A: Always the one being dumped. I could never pluck up the courage to dump anyone at all even though we were clearly incompatible, which is making me sound vastly nicer than I actually was. I didn't have the guts to finish with them; I just two-timed them all instead.

Q: Were you ever broken hearted?
A: Yes, but only because my pride was hurt. Getting dumped is infuriating. Apart from anything else, no-one ever believes you if you try to say that you had been trying to pluck up the courage to dump them for ages anyway.

The only time I have really been broken-hearted is when I have been dumped for another woman, which in reality is every time I suspect, but I always did the dumb thing of asking if there was someone else and then, when the answer was 'Yes', I always wanted to know who she was, how old she was, did I know her, how good-looking was she and crucially what was she like in bed? Some men who dumped me had the audacity and stupidity to tell me the (real) answers to those questions without cushioning me from more pain. They know who they are, and they deserve to feel ashamed. The answer to a wronged woman who asks about the sordid details of their new sex life with their new woman is to tell you nothing or lie.

But one day you meet someone who you don't want to dump (much) and who doesn't want to dump you (much). They are called THE ONE.

How do you know if someone is the one? There's no-one else left.
JENNY ECLAIR

4 · Passion
(or maybe not...)

MOVING ON – MOVING IN

The relationship is going well: you've met his parents and he's met yours, you've met some of his friends and on the whole they are all tolerable, you've sussed out his financial potential, he's sussed out or tried out your sexual potential, you've nursed one another through a bad cold, you've been camping in the Lake District for the weekend, you've seen each other in the bath, and you've even heard each other fart in the bath.

Sooner or later the idea of moving in together happens, or more accurately it occurs to her. Everyone else you know is starting to settle down, to pair up, and the idea of being in the dating game well into your thirties scares the pants off you (and so it should). Then there is your biological clock, which is decidedly ticking. So the process of becoming a (grumpy old) couple begins. She leaves some underwear or a t-shirt in his bedroom drawer, he then leaves a razor and a toothbrush at hers, you spend the weekend at his house and come home on a Sunday night to collect your stuff, and things go off in his fridge because he is always round at yours. Moving in makes sense, but then a lot of things make sense, like income tax, but it doesn't mean it is a good thing. Per se.

You could of course get married, but we've saved that treat for the next chapter.

Once you have decided to make a dishonest couple of each other, and your mother has cried with either shame or relief, there is the tricky decision of where to live. Does one of you give up your own place and scatter all your belongings conspicuously into your partner's, or do you get somewhere neutral that is a new place for both? Either way the woman is going to be in charge because on the whole, unless they're gay, men don't really give a toss whose sofa they are sitting on or whose curtains are hanging in the living room. They don't even notice bless them. However, there are some little tips/pointers we can offer, which may be worth bearing in mind during this phase of your relationship.

His or hers

Obviously making the choice between his and hers is simplified if he has a charming coach house with orchard and paddock, courtesy of some family legacy, and you have been living in a squat in Peckham. Ooh decisions, decisions. Equally if she has a loft conversion overlooking Tower Bridge and you've been living in your mate Damien's spare room for the last fifteen years it's easy.

However, for most couples choosing where to live is a minefield. This is probably where you will start using the dreaded word 'compromise'. All sorts of stuff needs to be taken into consideration: how long it will take either of you to get to work, proximity of parents (for him the further away the better), nearest decent supermarket/bars, parking implications, etc.

Location, location, location – what he wants

To be in staggering distance from a proper pub, i.e. a pub that has a darts board, quiz night, pool, pork scratchings, variety of beer called things like 'dog's breath' and 'brown moggy', plus a Sunday morning old-gits football team

A corner shop where he can buy emergency supplies, such as a
morning paper, a pint of milk, lavatory paper, Fray Bentos
pies and a pack of Guinness

He would rather it wasn't on the top of a hill in case he ever
actually takes up cycling, but the clincher would be off-street
parking. Every man should be entitled to his own driveway
even if he hasn't got a car

Location, location, location – what she wants

Close proximity to a gastropub, somewhere with a real log fire
that serves not only sausage and mash but exotic salads
involving pomegranate. This pub should have squishy sofas
preferably in beaten-up brown leather

An organic grocery shop – within a five-minute walk. Well, it's
nice to be able to buy carrots that taste like carrot and loaves
of bread with bits of olive and rosemary sticking out of
them, which cost over three quid

A nearby nicky nacky noo shop. Somewhere she can buy
birthday cards and scented candles; one of those shops that
sells glittery hair slides and all sorts of things you didn't
know you wanted but can easily spend eighty quid on

A nice park/heath/common on which to stroll. Maybe one day
dogs will come into the frame, or babies. Women like somewhere picturesque to notice the changing of the seasons;
this is because we like saying stuff like, 'Ooh look darling,
daffodils' and then we like quoting that first line of the
Wordsworth poem (which is the only bit we can remember)

Really good parks often have small art galleries, boating lakes
and outdoor Shakespeare evenings – hoorah

Good schools nearby. Even if you have no children of your own,
it's nice to know that the kiddies that might be walking past
your front door aren't going to be the type to drop burning
dog poo through your letter box

Good local transport links (a railway station and a bus stop), adequate street lighting (but not one that's going to shine a massive white beam into your bedroom all blooming night), and a healthy Neighbourhood Watch (as opposed to an unhealthy Neighbourhood Watch)

Pavements that aren't awash with dog crap, burger cartons and chewing gum

See how much more circumspect us girls are – and no, we don't care if there's access to cable locally. Once we move in together, we shan't be watching telly, we shall be chatting and enjoying companionable silences whilst we read or pursue hobbies.

Warning

Just remember, girls, go for what you want by all means but if you end up with all your needs ticked off, but it takes him two-and-a-half hours to get to work, it might backfire. There is a possibility that he will be late on so many occasions he will get the sack and you will end up having to pay all the mortgage. This will turn you into a naggy bitch, he, on the other hand, will become emasculated, retire to the sofa and spend his life watching daytime TV and eating out of tins.

Don't say we didn't warn you.

Moving into the ex's side of the bed

Of course practicalities sometimes demand that you have to move into the place where once the ex ate, slept and had sex with the woman/man you are now living with.

This can cause ructions as no matter how hard you/he tries to get rid of the previous cohabitee's presence there will be a leftover jar of hair product that will fill you full of self doubt, to the extent that you start having to accidentally smash mugs that he/she might have drunk out of. You will also start delving and rummaging, trying to find scraps of paper with their handwriting on, old photos, etc. In some cases this will lead to paranoid episodes of hearing the ex's voice and being able to 'feel' them in the house. For God's sake, if this happens, get some proper help. We don't know what to say for the best; we're out of our depth.

Building your own house

Don't. Your relationship is very new, so don't risk it by doing something that could very easily end in tears, bankruptcy and one of you running off with a Polish plumber. Remember, building your own house will mean living in a caravan for seven years until the damn thing is finished. Save building your own house for when the kids have grown up and left home and don't spoil things before they've even started.

CHOOSING THINGS

When choosing a sofa, let him have the last say. After all he's going to be the one sleeping on it.

Don't let her have an Aga, just because she wants one, unless you make sure she knows how to use the thing. If she's only used a microwave before, put your foot down, otherwise the two of you will end up starving to death.

He will want a Bang & Olufsen sound system. Now this is the sort of thing that can lead to her packing her bags and going home to mother. Men for some reason think it's alright to spend over £10,000 on a state-of-the-art sound system, women would rather eat their first-born than waste money like this. The fact is, women don't really listen to music; we don't mind something to sing along to on the car radio and we miss *Top of the Pops*, but spending money on stereos and such-like is plain silly. We know that once some state-of-the-art hi-fi stuff has been secreted into our walls, a radiator will spring a leak and the whole lot will have to come out. These are the sort of things we can predict, because deep down every woman is a witch.

Is he a snorer? Or she? If so then you will need to bear in mind strategies beyond upholstery choices and may need architectural ones. There are such things as double-door snorers, even double-floor snorers – and snoring, we are here to warn you, can only get worse with time. Men, especially Grumpy Old Men, snore so loudly they sound like hedge trimmers. Earplugs are not sufficient and sadly putting knitting needles up the offender's nostrils is not allowed.

Clothes

Once you are an officially cohabiting couple it is your right to interfere with his wardrobe. This is seldom a two-way street as men don't really notice what the love of their life is wearing. As long as she doesn't look like a hooker/Su Pollard/or a geography teacher, they don't really notice the subtleties.

This is not true of all men. Some blokes like their women to be 'snazzy dressers': this means high heels, handbags and lots of cleavage. This type of man expects grooming, which means nails (hands and toes) and hair; all this is fair enough if he's got the money and you've got the inclination. Unless you are really into playing trophy wife, there is something a bit vile about a man who can't love you for what you are, roots and all. However, on the other hand, it's a bit mean to capture your fellow by pretending to be something out of a forties Hollywood glamour movie only to revert to Mrs Slob as soon as you've bagsied him.

What we all need is a bit of compromise. Women: it's our duty to scrub up now and again. Men are naturally competitive, so if you're going to his office Xmas do, get the control pants and your glad rags on. You don't want to be the old boiler in the corner, nor do you want to look like an expensive whore – so be careful.

Hint

The high street shop Next is very good for that 'something in the middle' line and there's always good old Marks and Spencer's (what would we do without them? We'd be savages in horrible pants). Of course it's very galling for a woman to spend a huge amount of time and money on making themselves look present-able when the old man is oblivious.

A common scenario for most women is that they will spend seventy quid having their hair cut and blow dried and when you ask your partner what's different – he will wonder if you've bought a new sofa.

Remember: if you really want a bloke to notice what you're wearing then the answer is stockings.

Sorting out his appalling taste

Some men simply can't dress themselves. It's fine if they've got the sort of job that requires a suit as most men look OK in a suit. All you need to do is make sure he doesn't wear novelty ties or socks with cartoon characters on, and then you can let him out of the house.

It's at weekends that your love can really let you down. The biggest problems are horrible trainers, and baggy jogging bottoms that make him look like his crotch has dropped. Why do middle-aged men insist on dressing as if they are about to compete in some form of athletics track event when they are two stone over-weight and can't walk up a flight of stairs without clinging to the bannisters.

The trick of course is to 'accidentally on purpose' shrink every-thing you don't like and replace these hideous – but now doll-sized – items with things you do like. The shoe dilemma is more of a problem; I'd buy a puppy with a chewing fetish and train it to only eat hideous white trainers.

Women like men to wear polished leather shoes – not grey slip-ons.

Hair and grooming for men

Women prefer grey hair to dyed hair and no hair to comb-overs. We like clean fingernails and minimal jewellery. The only way men can get away with long hair (and possibly a ponytail), loads of bling and eye make-up is if they are a very famous rock star and – no – being in a pub band and singing cover versions of Rolling Stones hits doesn't count.

Tattoos are best kept off the knuckles and below the neckline.

Hair and grooming for women

Don't suddenly get your silky long hair cut. He won't think your new haircut is cutting-edge and funky; he will think you look like a lesbian and this will potentially cause him erectile dysfunction.

Complicated hairstyles requiring a great deal of lacquer will confuse him – keep it simple.

He will think your hair straighteners are tiny George Foreman grills, ideal for a small pork chop.

He will tell you he prefers you without any make-up but the day you don't put any on he will ask if you need to go to the doctor's because you look so ill.

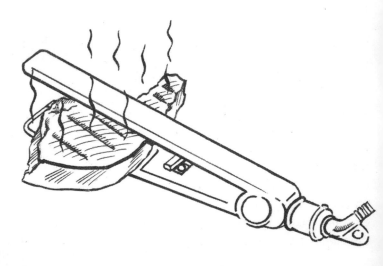

Other things to take into consideration on moving in with your chosen one

Or – how to make sure it's a love nest and not a war zone.

Thought: don't be mean. If you know he's asthmatic, do not buy goose-feather pillows and duvets. Yes, they may be more natural but there will be nothing natural about the ensuing wheezing.

On the other hand – if you are asthmatic and you move into her place and she's got a cat, well catty was there first – so tough.

Often, when you first move in, you get a bit of a nasty shock. For women it will dawn on them that the bloke they thought was 'the one and only' turns out not to be able to screw together a flat-pack IKEA shelving unit or change a light bulb, so yes, whilst he might be 'the one and only' she's still going to have to get another bloke in – one who knows one end of a screwdriver from another.

For blokes, despite the fact he thinks you're a goddess, he might have to come to terms with the fact that you're a goddess who doesn't believe in 'afters'.

Fact

Men don't think a yoghurt constitutes 'pudding'. They think 'pudding' means apple pie/crumble, spotted dick, jam roly poly – basically anything you can pour custard over.

THE UGLY TRUTH

It's at this stage that things start to go wrong in terms of the basic nuts and bolts of the relationship, and the passion and mystery go out of the window. Not totally. It might take a couple of months for you to start sitting on the loo in front of one another, but the crucial test is the farting one. This is a positive watershed. If you can't fart in front of one another you are frankly doomed. For one thing you are going to spend your whole life moving rooms or locking the bathroom door to let off, and this is going to be very annoying indeed.

> *The first time a girl farts in front of you is quite hideous really, isn't it? You know they do it and you don't really mind, but it's like ... keep it secret love, and don't waft. You know you're a flower, you're a princess, you're not me mate in the club, we're not playing snooker; don't fart and then grab me head. It's not right, is it?* JUSTIN MOORHOUSE

> *Romance goes out of the window the first time someone breaks wind and that's when you know when the relationship's going to be a goer or not, 'cos if he laughs and does it back then you know it's love. But if he looks genuinely appalled or pretends it hasn't happened, or leaves the room gagging, then you know you're not really compatible.* JENNY ECLAIR

You need to be able to embrace the losing of the mystery and, if you can't, you may as well forget it. Because although, yes, losing the mystery and seeing those intimate and horribly revealing habits they have is a bit like finding out there's no Father Xmas, until you have done so you are not truly a couple. Of course there are pros and cons to losing the mystery: on the one hand you have to face up to the fact that the special tube of ointment in the bathroom is for his big toe fungal nail infection, but on the other hand being able to slob about in your trackie bottoms with a bowl of leftover rhubarb crumble with a partner who doesn't pull a face is a very wonderful thing. As long as the pros outnumber the cons, there are many advantages to being a Grumpy Old Couple. Phew.

THE UPSIDE OF BEING IN A LONG-TERM RELATIONSHIP

If you are going to be in a long-term relationship you might as well reap the benefits. Enjoy some of the things, or some would say the only things, that are good:

You can stay in on a Saturday night and no-one cares

You can walk to the bath without having to hold your stomach in

You can have someone to sit next to when you have your tea in front of the telly on a tray – bliss

You can go for a long walk with someone, enjoy the fresh air without looking like a total saddo and yet not have to make polite conversation

You can go on holiday and not have to make polite conversation at all, or indeed any conversation visible to the naked eye

You don't have to get dressed, get in the car and drive all the way home in the middle of the night because you have to be at work early the next day

You can have an early night without it turning into a sex marathon

He's seen you in your glasses so you don't have to wear contact lenses all the time

You don't have to wear high heels

There is someone to take the hit when you get caught speeding on that same camera again and you can pretend that it was your partner who was speeding not you, depending on who has the most penalty points

But the downside is you have to make sure you've made a sensible choice of long-term partner.

HOW TO SPOT IF YOU'VE MOVED IN WITH A PSYCHO

The day they move in they bring out their collection of
    Churchill's speeches on vinyl

They hide when someone rings the door bell

They pretend they are away on a sales conference when their
    mother plans to come and stay

They have to have all the towels straight in the bathroom and all
    the tins in the cupboard colour-coded. Apparently David
    Beckham suffers from domestic OCD; ah yes, but on the
    plus side it's David Beckham. He can straighten my towels
    and rearrange my cupboards any old day – phnaaargh

They talk back to the television, i.e. when Fiona Phillips says
    'Good morning' they respond with a cheery 'Good morning
    Fiona'

You look out of the window and they are doing tai chi in the
    garden; when you laugh, they are really offended

They curtain twitch like an old woman and provide a running
    commentary about what the neighbours are doing, 'Well
    she's late again and she's worn that skirt four times on
    the trot'

They leave out saucers of milk and scraps for the foxes

They set the table for breakfast the night before

BEWARE POLITICS AND RELIGION – AND MORE

It might not be until you move in with each other that you realise
that you have fundamental problems with your views on the big
stuff. Whilst you are dating you will have discussed your favourite
movies, the toss-up between Thai and Indian, red wine versus
white wine, but you might not realise until it's slightly too late that
one of you is a fully paid-up card-carrying New Labourite whilst

the other buys the *Daily Mail*. Other political problems can also arise: one of you is green to the point of having a wormery, the other drives a Bentley.

And religious discrepancies ... for example, she might be a devout *X Factor* fan whilst you've converted to *Dancing on Ice*, Just don't let this get out of hand, as it has been known to cause huge family rifts.

The thing is, before you settle down properly with each other, you are so busy having sex that you don't notice that she thinks two baths a day is normal, leaves the landing light on all night, has the tumble drier set on constant, would rather put the central heating on than another jumper and throws plastic bags straight in the garbage.

Young people are much more energy aware than us old farts. I know of a couple who split up because she didn't buy energy-efficient light bulbs!

Lark or owl?

This is another thing you might not really know about each other. There is nothing more irritating for a lark than to get lumbered with someone who can barely grunt before midday and thinks a coffee and a cigarette constitutes breakfast.

Conversely, there is nothing more galling for the owl than to get stuck with someone who likes to have the bedside light off by ten and gets weepy if you're still up listening to music at 3 a.m.

One lump or two?

It's tricky when there's only one lump in the relationship as it leads to guilt, lies and deceit.

Basically, the sporty and the non-sporty should leave each other alone; it's not going to work. Hell hath no greater fury than the lump pushed out of bed to go for an early-morning jog.

On the whole, exercise, unless your partner shares the same enthusiasm, should be considered very similar to masturbation:

a necessary evil to be practised privately and never referred to over the supper table.

That said, even the most evenly matched sporty couple can jeopardise their relationship by playing games together. Table tennis in my experience can become really quite competitive and nasty, as can any bat and ball combo. Thing is, with the bat and the ball, you've got two weapons. He will try to take your eye out with the ball and you will accidentally on purpose try to hit him hard round the back of the head with the bat.

Even board games can turn nasty. Men like to abide by the rules, whereas women think cheating should be allowed if the game needs to be over so that she can set the table for supper.

Of course there is always going to be trouble if both of you have been used to playing with the little silver top hat. You can't both have your own way.

Actually, come to think of it, this is a phrase that needs to be incorporated into every marriage ceremony: 'and remember, you can't both have your own way' – so make sure you're quick and get your way first girls.

SEX IN A LONG-TERM RELATIONSHIP

I've been with the same man for twenty-five years. Twenty-five years of sharing the same bed. He has it Mondays, Wednesdays and Fridays.   JENNY ECLAIR

Obviously once people live together and can therefore have sex together as much as they like, they don't; they stop. The reason that marriage or cohabiting (to give it that cute title) works at all is that it has a winning combination – maximum of opportunity coupled with the minimum of temptation (George Bernard Shaw).

People obviously endlessly lie about their sex lives. One recent US study found that men had an average of seven sex partners in their lives and that women had an average of four. Another study in *The Times* by British researchers stated that men had 12.7 heterosexual partners and women 6.5. So someone, somewhere, along the line is fibbing ... do the maths. Anyway, what are those .5s all about? Are we having sex with people who can only count as half human? Oh listen, we've all made mistakes.

> *If you're having good sex it's not as important as the other things.*
> *If you're having bad sex or no sex it actually poisons the rest of the*
> *relationship. Try not having sex and then just see how you feel.*
> TRACEY COX

Women tend to view sex a bit like housework: a quick but thorough tidy once a week, with a full-blown spring clean once a year.

Men tend to view sex in ... magazines, which they hide in their shed and feel bad about. Women's pornography on the other hand includes magazines such as *Heat, Hello!, Take a Break* and *OK!*

OVER-FAMILIARITY

Once you've moved in together, unless you are very rigid and prim about it, all sorts of bodily functions will rise to the surface for the other one to see. Things that you kept hidden, like how greedy you are with your food, or how you bleach your moustache or that you wear corrective underwear are now evident for your partner to see.

> *There is such a thing as familiarity breeding contempt. Don't let*
> *them in the bathroom when you are on the toilet, don't let them*
> *see you with your moustache bleach over your mouth. Our*
> *mothers always used to tell us that kind of thing and we said,*
> *'Oh it's modern now, we don't have to be like that'... but you*
> *know you kind of do.* JENNI TRENT HUGHES

For starters, he will see you without your make-up on. Back in the fifties, women used to set their alarms deliberately early so that they could creep out of bed and 'put on their face', so as not to frighten their husband and put him off his full English breakfast. I'm really surprised that at some point, someone didn't invent 'face enamelling', but no, women have become increasingly sloppy about maintaining their allure.

Grooming has gone out of the window, no-one has a 'shampoo and set' any more, we've given up on stockings, our shoes no longer match our handbags, we've chucked our girdles and to be honest most women these days wake up covered in shaving stubble with the appalling breath of a badly constipated bison.

You really know when you're a Grumpy Old Couple when you're not sneaking off to the bathroom every five minutes to clean your teeth. Back when you were 'courting' you were obsessive about fresh breath; all those discreet little extra strong mints, the mini sprays of 'gold spot' and worrying about ordering anything that might contain garlic. Once you move in together, those worries are the thing of the past and six months down the line cleaning your teeth counts as foreplay.

There is also a huge change in the way that men and women eat in front of one another. On the first date they normally pick at their food (this is obviously true of women), on the second they do actually read the menu, and on about the tenth date a woman just might eat some chips, although even then she won't have ordered them. By the time you have moved in with one another, however, your ability to cram three Jaffa Cakes into your mouth in one go – and your Bakewell tart addiction – is hard to hide.

What's really annoying is when your partner isn't as greedy as you are. By rights men should be the greediest in a relationship, what's quite shocking for a lot of women is that quite often they aren't. Men tend to get hungry, eat something, feel full and stop. For women eating is much more complicated than simply satisfying hunger.

For some reason women will stuff themselves, feel guilty, promise to go on a diet tomorrow and tiptoe down the stairs at five minutes to midnight to have a quick poached egg. Many women, when caught by their partners at the fridge midnight feasting, will pretend to be sleep walking.

Greed is an unattractive quality, but it is fairly infectious.

Eventually 'having a really good time in bed' will constitute snuggling under the duvet eating a Chinese takeaway whilst watching *The Talented Mr Ripley* – marvellous. Conversely being 'bad' in bed will be more about spilling a glass of Ribena than sexual prowess.

How long does romance last in a relationship? Until one of you breaks wind. Farting will happen more frequently and more loudly. One night you will have too much to drink and one or other of you will (if you love them) have to hold their head while they are sick. This is a true test of love and courage and is a fairly good indication as to whether you are going to be able to hack having kids.

THE EVERYDAY NITTY GRITTY

Once you are living together day in, day out, noticing each other's habits is unavoidable, and your patience can be stretched by the strangest of things – the way he holds his knife or the fact she has a funny sniff.

Other annoying habits that can start to grate

Whistling and humming
Leaving lids off ink pens
Hiding apple cores in a tissue under the sofa
Eating all the red ice lollies in the freezer and leaving all the
    yellow ones
Putting empty Marmite jars back in the cupboard

Saying, 'Well it wasn't me because I don't even eat Marmite'

Not liking Marmite

Liking marmalade more than Marmite

Buying marmalade but not Marmite

Saying, 'Why don't you try some marmalade?'

When you have just discovered that there is an empty jar of Marmite in the cupboard and HER toast is getting cold

Trimming toe nails over the loo but allowing them to ping all over the bathroom and then not picking any of them up because you think they all went down the loo and didn't bother to check

Leaving pans to soak when washing them up would have been entirely possible

Leaving the car without any petrol in

THE CHORES

Housework

The way it works with housework is that on the whole women do it and men don't. At least men do it when asked or urged or bribed (see sports section), otherwise they don't see the mess, or they say they are going to do it but haven't got round to it yet, which is code for they are going to leave it until you can stand it no more and get on and do it yourself. I know their little tricks. They had apparently got it all sussed when they were students ... boys in a flat-share would niftily sidestep all such work saying it didn't bother them that you had to wash up before you could cook or it didn't bother them that no-one had changed the sheets, or no-one had swept the kitchen floor, because they didn't notice anyway, so why would you mind? So women, if they wanted these things done, had to decide whether to do them themselves, and because their mothers instilled into them that their houses and homes should run shipshape (probably), and because their mothers liked to be

straight, they gave in. They are wired that way. It's true some women are wired in a different way, and I envy them if they don't give a stuff about it, and some men are wired in a different way, in which case I obviously should have married one. Either way the whole business of who takes out the kitchen bin and when, who makes the beds, who puts a wash on in the morning is a battleground. And once you have children magnify this battleground by 100%.

Of course the trick once you've had children is to wire them up to be obsessive cleaning freaks. A friend of mine's mum devised a game for her children whereby they played 'ladies and servants' and basically the kids cleaned the house while the mum lay on the sofa issuing orders in a comedy posh voice – clever.

What experienced Grumpy Old Couples tend to do is to out-martyr each other and play 'tired trumps'. (This, for once, has nothing to do with farting.)

TIRED TRUMPS: A PLAY FOR MARRIED PEOPLE

WIFE God I'm tired, I've been on my feet all day.

HUSBAND Well, I've been stuck in traffic and I didn't have time for lunch.

WIFE Lunch! I had a Ryvita whilst I did the ironing and now I suppose you expect me to cook something for dinner?

HUSBAND Actually I'm too tired to even think about eating.

WIFE I don't think I could even keep my eyes open to see what was on the plate, never mind lift a fork to my mouth, I'm that tired.

HUSBAND I'm so knackered I think I'll just go straight to bed.

WIFE I'm too tired to get up the stairs. I'll just sleep here, right here on the carpet.

HUSBAND OK, goodnight. (*Husband goes off to bed.*)

(*Wife raids fridge: eats a pork pie, some Brie, a leftover falafel and a chocolate mousse and then creeps up to bed where husband is snoring his head off.*)

Morning

WIFE Oh God, I didn't get a wink of sleep all night what with your snoring. I'm exhausted.

(*Repeat, until unconscious.*)

If you are already playing these sorts of games early on in your relationship, congratulations – you could almost skip the next chapter about weddings and move onto Chapter 6: Resignation the rot sets in.

THE TELLY

Despite the fact that when you are young and in love you reckon you'll be too busy having sex to watch telly, don't underestimate the lure of *Match of the Day*. Yes, you might be making love on the sofa, but see the way he's positioned you! Yes, you are doing it 'that way' so that he can satisfy you and watch Manchester v Chelsea.

Men, if they want to last the course, must realise that talking about buying a new car or getting a bigger mortgage is not allowed during soaps, bonnet dramas, reality TV shows and anything about fashion or babies.

RIGHTS TO THE BATHROOM

A woman has more right to the bathroom than a man, and it's a gentleman's duty to accept second go. If this means soggy towels, steamed up mirrors, shaving stubble all over the shop and scuzzy leftover bath water, then so be it. This is a right that must be exerted very early on in a relationship and should be honoured until neither of you are capable of self-abluting. We bear children; the least you can do is not complain about grey pubes in the soap.

SHARED CARS

Hmm, tricky one. Most people go for the take-it-in-turn thing, especially when it comes to the 'who stays sober this time?' argument. The trick to getting off with less than your fair share of staying sober, girls, is to be a really bad driver. He won't be able to stand it. All you need do is leave the handbrake on a couple of times, run out of oil/petrol and refuse to drive at more than 20 mph and, hey presto, all your driving obligations are null and void.

COOKING

When you first move in together you will make a real effort. The woman will pour over recipe books and set the table with candles and coasters, he will be appreciative and compliment the cook with every mouthful. A few years down the line you are eating Marks and Spencer's lasagnes off your knees in front of the telly. He's in the sitting room watching Charley Boorman and Ewan McGregor doing some daft road trip on motorbikes, while you are in the spare room watching *Cranford* in black and white. Tut.

Men can and will cook – and are often very good cooks, which tends to spoil the meal for a woman. Men don't tend to use recipe books; they just make it up as they go along – again this is very annoying.

Woman, despite being more experienced around the kitchen, will occasionally make stupid mistakes, like remembering to set the timer on the oven but not putting the oven on. This is infuriating, especially when it's a dreary November day and you're really looking forward to tucking into a lovely Delia casserole. There is nothing more annoying than hearing the oven timer beeping, only to open the door and find your dish stone cold and full of raw meat. He will use this as an excuse to go out and get cod and chips which is what he really wanted all along. Gggrrrrrr.

5 · Grumpy Old Weddings

Two out of three marriages end in divorce and the other one ends in murder but you know, everyone lives in eternal hope that we can find somebody that makes us happy for ever. JEFF GREEN

It seems that however much we know that weddings are a complete and utter waste of time we are still suckers for them. When it comes to weddings none of us seems able to cling on to logic or sense at all. This is because women have played being brides since they were four, and men don't have much choice in the matter.

The fact is that lots of girls still dream of having a white wedding. I suppose it's because – since they've done everything else – the only novelty left is to play virgins for the day.

Personally I can't be doing with people who opt for a religious ceremony despite the fact that the last time they were on hallowed ground was when they were fifteen and drinking cider in a graveyard – but I would say that, wouldn't I? It's the sort of thing Grumpy Old Women say.

*The trouble is, I reckon a lot of young women can't tell the differ-
ence between matrimony and a Disney cartoon. They don't want
to be a bride, they want to be a princess, complete with coach and
horses and a lot of daft nonsense if you ask me.*   JENNY ECLAIR

OK, so there are lovely moments in every wedding – like seeing
your loved one looking all fabulously fairy-like and beautiful and
rosy-cheeked and virginal walk down the aisle, or like being the
centre of attention for an entire day, or seeing your friends and
family cheer you on your wedded-bliss way, or seeing your grannie
look a bit tiddly and like you made her decade, or seeing rosebud
bouquets on the edge of a beautiful village church pew. Trouble is
these little moments of happiness take most people an entire year
to plan and easily an entire year to pay for. And for what? Once
you are a Grumpy Old Woman you don't even look back upon your
wedding day necessarily with that much affection, and you certainly don't look back at the photos at all, because for one thing
you looked so much skinnier and younger, and secondly it just
reminds you how long you have had to put up with one another.
The decision you made several decades ago to marry someone
seems now like it was made by someone entirely different living
a previous life. That's because you were a different person and you
were living a previous life. People change as they get older, a lot.
So you have to embrace the change in one another or build an
extension so that you don't have to see one another so often.

   Depressing ? No not really – just realistic. OK, so there are one
or two couples that you look at and think that they have a fabulously loving relationship or that they have a special chemistry.
You probably even cite them in marital arguments and say, 'Look
how loving Richard always is to Penelope,' or, 'Look how Penelope
butters Richard's toast for him – why don't you do that for me?'
And then invariably you hear that they have split up. They are
usually the ones who go off with their painter and decorator or
shack up with their PA. The grass is never as green as you think

it is with other couples. The truth is staying hitched up with someone for decades is jolly hard work.

In the olden days the only way of guessing how your partner was going to deteriorate was to check out their mum and dad. Not any more. Scientific advancement means there's a new piece of Photoshop software that shows you what your spouse might look like in fifty years' time. You simply scan in a recent photograph and, hey presto, with the press of a button you can see her – digitally aged, all fat and whiskery – with a face that is so jowelly it looks like it needs scaffolding.

If you're doing this experiment together, try not to scream when you see what you're going to get lumbered with– and remember, cosmetic surgery is getting cheaper by the day.

But let's go back to the original decision in the first place ...

WHEN YOU SHOULD HEAR ALARM BELLS RINGING

Don't marry anyone if they:

Personalise their voice mail

Wear underwear that is more than five years old (but you can guarantee that once you have married them they will indeed be wearing underwear at least this old and so will you)

Have odd ex girlfriends

Have more than two ex wives; two marriages is a pity, three is frankly careless

Keep photos of ex's and ex's letters, and especially don't marry them if you find a file with them all sorted by surname

Exfoliate (women are allowed to do this, men aren't)

Make jokes about your nose or call it a hooter

Slap you on the bottom like a horse

Don't know one end of a Hoover from another

Have a (very) annoying mother

On the other hand some of the positive reasons for getting married are:

He's got a decent pension

He will drive when you want to drink

There will be someone there to bring you grapes in hospital when you are very old and most of your friends have pegged it

Everyone needs someone to take the bins out when you are not at home

Putting duvet covers on without help is a pain in the neck

CIVIL PARTNERSHIPS

There is a huge problem about what you call someone that you're with but aren't actually married to. Being gay there is a particular problem with civil partnerships. I have a civil partner. It sounds awful, it sounds so municipal but I hate words like other half. I tend to say what is the truth – my best friend.
MATTHEW PARRIS

What do you call yourself if you're a couple but not married? Happy. BRIAN CONLEY

These days it is very old fashioned to get married in the conventional way. People have civil partnerships, or blessings or civic ceremonies in grand hotels or stately homes, or they get married on a beach in Jamaica or in Vegas or in Colwyn Bay because it's ironic. Which is fine and dandy – but mostly for the loving couple, not for the guests who have to fly to Jamaica or Vegas or indeed drive to Colwyn Bay to witness the blessing of their relationship. Trouble is now that we know that so many marriages end in divorce we are a teeny bit meaner and more sceptical about the whole process. I suppose some weddings are rock solid: the ones based on tax relief, or with prenuptial agreements, or indeed the rare ones which are based on two people being utterly besotted with one another ... But the rest are basically expensive showing off.

CIVIL CEREMONIES

Civil ceremonies now account for three-fifths of all weddings, and a quarter take place in approved venues rather than registry offices. Young couples marrying for the first time often like to have a church wedding, but only 14% of couples who are remarrying choose a church venue. If people choose to marry in a non-church setting, there is a rather draconian rule that prevents them from having any religious overtones at all in their ceremony – no prayers, bless-ings, hymns or bible readings ... which seems a bit harsh. No wonder we are now apparently the most secular nation on earth.

What prospective parents of the bride and groom have to realise is that weddings have gone show bizzy in recent years and they are not the simple operations they were in our day. Not that weddings have ever been simple but once upon a time your choice was either the church or the registry office. There was none of this gallivanting off to Antigua or sky-diving out of a plane together. Nowadays the choice is mind-boggling, although more and more people are what our mothers would call 'shacking up together'. Weddings are enjoying a bit of a renaissance and people are tying the knot in increasingly odd ways. More bizarre/interesting venues include:

London and Edinburgh zoos
Racecourses (Bath's said to be the best because it has a great
    backdrop)
The London Eye
The Editor's office at the *Daily Mirror*
The Natural History Museum

Summit of the Cairngorms (also Snowdon, various peaks in the
    Lakes, etc.)
Football grounds – Sheffield Wednesday was one of the first.
    Tottenham is also a popular one. Often guests come to the
    wedding dressed in the club's colours, and football songs
    are sung instead of more traditional wedding songs
Coronation Street set (particularly popular for gay civil
    partnerships)
PizzaExpress in Stirling
Harvey Nichols in Edinburgh (the first store in Scotland to
    get a wedding licence)
Prison
Hospital

Asda in York was one of the first supermarkets to host a wedding,
in February 2004. The lucky couple got married there with
ten bridesmaids in attendance

And for the really adventurous:

Underwater using scuba-diving equipment
Mid-air with parachutes
Wing-walking: for this you need two planes. The person officiat-
ing is strapped to the wing of the aeroplane in front: the
happy couple are on either wing of the second plane. Vows
have to be done through a microphone because of the noise
of the plane and the wind

Personally I think making such a hoo hah might be covering up
some fundamental lack of excitement within the relationship itself
– but then I'm not Marj Proops (showing my age there) so what
do I know?

In spite of the vast choice available, it appears that, increasingly, more people are choosing to just get married at home.

NEW GAY WEDDING LAW – 2005

Gay weddings became legal in Northern Ireland on 19 December
2005, in Scotland on 20 December 2005 and in England and Wales
on 21 December 2005 – like a big Mexican wave of camp solidarity.
One of the first same-sex couples to tie the knot were Elton John
and David Furnish at Windsor Guildhall; earlier in the year, Charles
and Camilla had used the same venue but didn't spend nearly as
much on flowers, obviously. The ceremony can take place at any
premises approved for marriage, and legally the relationship is
recognised in much on flowers, the same way as a heterosexual
marriage. Brighton had the highest number of gay weddings in
the first few months – 510 in the first two months alone – and it's

estimated that 4,500 gay couples had a civil partnership in the first year of legislation in the UK.

It is now illegal for shops to refuse to have wedding gift lists for gay couples (although why they would in the first place is anyone's guess, especially since I imagine the list is longer, more expensive and easily more exacting than most heterosexual ones).

Weddings have always been big business, and are even bigger now that our lesbian sisters and homosexual brothers are allowed in on the act. Personally I'm all in favour of gay civil partnerships – even though the word 'civil partnership' sounds more like a contract to build a municipal library rather than anything that might involve confetti. Apart from the human rights angle, I don't see why the parents of gay kids should get off scot-free when it comes to the headache and trauma of arranging a wedding.

PRENUPTIAL AGREEMENTS

I think there is a case for these, but rather than simply being financial arrangements perhaps these should apply to the more important factors which to a Grumpy Old Couple are likely to be very significantly divisive. In other words, we should have certain things banned legally in a marriage contract. Obviously you can custom build your own clauses, but the following might be interesting food for thought for a possible prenuptial list:

Irritating eating habits will – and can – only get worse – not better – with fewer teeth and less vanity; eating separately might be the way forward

Washing up and cleanliness habits in the kitchen can be surprisingly tricky for a couple that has been cohabiting for longer even than *Big Brother* has been on the telly. His habit of leaving things to soak may now send a Grumpy Old Woman near to breaking point, but on the other hand Grumpy Old

Men can go the other way; they can get very fussy and old womanish about the washing-up and kitchen routines. My Grumpy Old Man has started getting very fussy indeed about rinsing everything before it goes into the dishwasher, and also has developed hideously complex stacking routines. If things aren't stacked by others 'properly' he gets it all out again and restacks, all presumably motivated by wanting to save money (his overriding motivation with everything as it happens), so most of the time the things that are dirty and waiting to be washed in the dishwasher are actually all over the work surfaces waiting to go back in a more organised order

Personal hygiene. Dental floss should be written into the prenuptial

Snoring – this like everything can only get worse – for her and him

Bad presents – like kitchen utensils or car accessories – should carry heavy punishment

Conversely, women should expect to lose out financially should they commit any of the following crimes against matrimony:

Forgetting, completely and utterly, what his golf handicap is

Hiding new shoes on top of the wardrobe and then lying and saying you 'bought them in the sale'

Telling your girlfriends about his oddly shaped testicles and then falling about laughing

Making him go shopping/to the theatre more times than is natural for any man

Scraping his car and then making matters worse by trying to fill in the scratch really badly with nail varnish

But back to the romantic bit ...

THE PROPOSAL

I actually proposed to my wife dressed as a knight in armour on a white charger because I thought, 'If I am going to do it, I might as well do it good.' She didn't even say 'Yes'. She just screamed and ran off. BRIAN CONLEY

The way my husband proposed to me was quite romantic. We'd already had our first child, we were living together and I wasn't really expecting to marry him ... and I got home from work and on our dining-room table was a registry office booking form with a Post-it note on it saying, 'I'm going to be there, will you?' I think that's quite romantic. TANYA BYRON

Every woman is partial to a proposal – it is written into our genes. The more romantic it is the more likely we are to say 'Yes'; we can't help it. We like proposals to feature expensive hotels, candlelit dinners, romantic sunsets on Caribbean beaches, etc. We emphatically do not want to be proposed to in the pub or at Tesco, even though it seems amusing. Amusing is very bad. Romantic and sloppy is good. You may as well savour the romance and make the most of it now because, let's be honest, the moment you decide to get married it changes. The gloves are off.

In fact the gloves probably come off minutes after he has gone down on one knee – and is struggling to get back up. At this point you will think, 'Oh, for heaven's sake man, do you need to make such a song and dance about everything; can't you get up without your knee ricocheting out of its socket?'

THE RING THING

Before women became such terrible control freaks, men used to surprise them with an engagement ring in a little velvet box. Nowadays women choose their own and all the element of surprise is gone. This is because women don't like surprises and neither do they like playing 'Hunt the Engagement Ring', so gentlemen should avoid hiding it.

But if you must hide it, traditional surprise hiding places for the engagement ring include: in a glass of champagne, secreted within a Christmas cracker and tucked into an oyster. However, tucking an expensive engagement ring into an oyster can have appalling consequences, involving a long wait and a rubber glove.

ENGAGEMENT

Getting engaged seems to have gone out of fashion entirely, which is a shame because it was a good idea, if only because it had a very practical purpose: namely to prompt a round of expensive presents that was far enough away from the wedding to mean you got two bites at it … and normally it involved a nice ring, a nicer ring in fact than the wedding ring, given that it should by rights contain a very large sapphire or diamond or both.

The only downside to getting engaged is that you have to find a way of referring to one another: that is, not fiancé, which clearly is a silly word which makes people, especially men, look absurdly mumsy.

Obviously engagement parties with loads of presents for our generation was a good idea, but for today's youth I don't think so. You couldn't trust young people these days not to be silly about the presents. Can you imagine how many daft lads would try and sneak a new PlayStation 3 plus loads of games onto the list?

THE STAG NIGHT

Stag nights have become huge production numbers. Way back in the Dark Ages stag nights just involved blokes, they got drunk down the local pub and larked about a bit. Granted they had a hangover for the day itself, which every bride finds hard to come to terms with (especially if it involves the bridegroom either being sick or oversleeping and forgetting to put those nice shoes on she wanted him to wear) ... but back then they didn't cost almost as much as the wedding itself. OK, so occasionally the bridegroom's mates organised a couple of strippers, got him pissed, and tied him to the lamp post with only a jar of peanut butter to cover his decency. Nowadays, it's at least a weekend, it's fifteen blokes going to Prague and attempting to shag enough women to make monogamy seem like a well-earned rest.

THE HEN NIGHT

Similarly, this used to be a crowd of girls having a pizza and a carafe of wine to toast the bride-to-be's future. Not any more. Oh no, these days it's got to be a weekend break that includes at least three of the following things:

A pamper session
Go-karting
VIP entry to a nightclub
Clay pigeon shooting
Pole dancing
A ride in a stretch limo
Someone waving a dildo
Dressing up with L-plates and fairy wings
Tequila shots issued by a girl wearing a shots belt like a holster,
    who gets aggressive if the shots aren't downed in one
White-water rafting
Customised t-shirts with stuff like '100% up for it' written on
    the front, or 'Kell's hen party member – please put into
    recovery position if found in gutter'

I promise you, there are vast numbers of websites begging to take
your money and send you paintballing in Tallinn. Seriously, you
can also go to Budapest and learn to shoot KGB-style (true). Who
said romance was dead?

Of course the only thing most hen parties can guarantee is a
stinking hangover. I once sat on a plane coming back to the UK
from Prague. Apart from me and my daughter everyone else on
the plane had been to a stag or hen do. Without exception they
were all shivery with tiredness and the smell of stale vomit and
despair was palpable. Tut and double tut.

THE WEDDING LIST

Twenty years ago your said 'toaster' or 'Goblin teasmade'. Now
people have the cheek to ask for presents from some smart shop and
the cheapest item is twelve silver-plated knives from the designer
range priced £350 and, guess what, all the cheap stuff gets ticked off
by the richest of the guests who are smart enough to get down to the

store as soon as the invite arrives. By the time you get to look into what's left of the Royal Doulton they like, all the eggcups and cheap things have gone, and it's only the large dinner plates or expensive soup tureen that haven't been 'bagsied'.

Wedding presents are of course the real point of weddings. When you have lost touch with the bridesmaids, given the dress away to Oxfam and have twenty-five years of marriage on the clock, some of the wedding presents are still going strong, probably stronger than your relationship in fact ... And here's the thing: as long as you have been married for five years or so you get to keep the presents even if the marriage falls apart. (Anything less than five years is a bit dodgy present-wise.) Given that a vast amount of marriages do end in divorce, this is an important fact when considering marriage in the first place. By the way, cohabitees don't get much in the way of presents.

Even greedier are those couples who beg for money because they are 'saving up for a new kitchen'. Well, if a kitchen was that vital, you could have done without the vodka luge and the £17,000 firework display, which everyone had to hang around till midnight for – tut, it's just getting silly. I wouldn't mind, but is anyone writing thank-you letters for all these demands – whoops ... I mean gifts?

Thing is, when these marriages go tits up, do we get our gifts back? No, we don't and let's face it, a lot of presents that we bought are still under guarantee. When the marriage hits the rocks, we could take them back and get a refund. It's the selfishness that gets me.

THE COST TO THE GUEST

Being a guest at a wedding these days costs a fortune. Often you have to go to Barcelona for the hen or stag weekend, you have to buy a new outfit, pay for the family to stay in a posh hotel and buy everyone drinks that cost more than you could have imagined. All this and then you have to sit next to someone's maiden Aunt Doris.

If you have been chosen as a bridesmaid you can double the trouble. For a start you are going to have to wear a hideous figure-hugging dress, you will be expected to buy more drinks than anyone at the hen do, you are going to have to have your hair and make-up done professionally, you will have to lose weight, go on a pamper day and be very, very nice to the bride's mother who is in a panic for a full month in the run-up to the Big Day.

If you are best man you can write off the best part of a month's salary and you can count on spending most of your annual leave going up and down to the village church in Hertfordshire for meetings with the vicar and the wedding planner, and organising car parking and ceremony rehearsals. All this and the loving couple will probably end up being married for only a couple of years anyway.

THE SEATING PLAN

The wedding seating plan is easily the biggest nightmare of the whole shebang and easily the worst problem of logistics you are ever likely to have to solve. Aunty Beatty hasn't spoken to the rest of the family for years, but how can you seat her next to anyone from his side when she is so hideously unsociable? And in any case they all live in Kent and if you sit her next to them she will realise that you drive past her house at least once a month and never drop in. No, the whole thing is disastrously complex, and can only lead to someone being very, very upset indeed. Some people are brave enough to take on a top table system to boot, with the best man, bridesmaids and bride and bridegroom's (blood) parents – a recipe for violence once the drink has kicked in. A buffet is probably the answer.

Of course you could throw caution to the wind and do without place names and a seating plan altogether – what a blessed relief! All the oldies will gather at the oldie tables and moan about the cutlery not being particularly well polished, whilst all the youngies will gang up together and take drugs. Aunty Beatty will sit by herself – good, serve the old bag right.

THE WEDDING DRESS

Wedding dresses are by definition a teensy bit too small and a teensy bit too over-the-top. You are only going to wear it once, so what on earth is the point of paying over a thousand pounds for it (spend it on some good linen or bedding)? In fact, here's to Primark selling them in some nice classic designs that won't date but will last for one (long) day. Men would like that because they could be given permission to rip them off at the end of the wedding day for the consummation of the marriage, which is the bit they look forward to all day anyway.

WEDDINGS – THE FEMALE PERSPECTIVE

For some women their wedding day was and remains the best day of their life. For others passing their driving test was more of a buzz. Here are some emotions a woman feels on her wedding day:

A bit sick, which is why she should never have a Bucks Fizz, the most acidic drink in the world. The last thing we want is for the bride to be burping at the altar. Stick to something milky – with a vodka chaser

A bit pre-menstrual: this might be hormones, in which case the honeymoon is going to be a right laugh – or nerves

The thing about wearing white is that even though you're not due for a fortnight the fact you're wearing white makes a period inevitable. Leaking on your wedding day is something no bride wants to worry about – 79% do *

A bit tired. In fact the prospect of the whole day with her hair scraped back in the vice-like grip of a thousand pins and keeping her tummy in is a bit daunting. There is a moment when every bride would rather forget the whole thing, put her dressing gown back on and watch telly with a cup of tea

Slightly worried about the groom's chin – it's a bit small

Claustrophobic. Many brides feel the urge to bolt on their wedding day. This is why the veil and train were introduced: to make it harder for her to 'get the hell out of there'.

Nervous about his speech; he's not very bright or funny

A bit concerned about the wedding night; the last time they did 'it' was a disaster

* From the Institute of Made-up Statistics

WEDDINGS – THE MALE PERSPECTIVE

Here are some things a groom might feel on his wedding day:

Hungover. The stag do was a week ago, but there are still some blanks that could do with filling in, like how come he was found tied to a rugby post in Cardiff?

A bit hungry – men are always hungry – what's new? Might as well take advantage of his mum bustling around and order another bacon sandwich. She will tell him not to get tomato ketchup on his shirt; he will get tomato ketchup on his shirt

Slightly pissed off that he's going to miss quite an important European Cup quarter-final. That's the trouble with having to book so far ahead, you never know what you're going to miss out on

Slightly in love with someone else: one of the bridesmaids, her auntie, that slaggy barmaid, the woman that works in the building society – just about everyone and anyone, apart from his betrothed

A bit worried about the wedding night as she's turning out not to be much of a 'goer'. The way things are going he's going to die before he's ever had a blow job.

Maybe he should stop the wedding car and visit that girl who will do them for a Crunchie bar on the way to the church?

BRIDESMAIDS

Bridemaids' dresses are by definition frou frou frilly and pointless; and face it, when you think you might wear it to an evening do some other time, you are kidding yourself. You can tell whether an evening dress is a recycled bridesmaid's dress because it has very obvious bust darts and is made from silky clingy material. Sometimes it is bright peach. Enough said. Plus, unless you are seven years old, if you are a bridesmaid you are going to be charged with looking after the little bridesmaids or page boys who will have toddler tantrums in the church or decide to steal the show or tread on your dress, or run amok in the church, and you won't be able to belt the little sods because too many people will be looking. The one good thing about being a bridesmaid is that you are expected to get off with someone at some point during the day (ideally not the groom), and there is usually a potential romantic development or three – presumably because all men find bridesmaids' dresses and bust darts a positive turn-on and they all secretly want to shag virgins. Either that or being a bridesmaid is so horribly trying that every bridesmaid eventually gets too drunk to care who chats them up.

THE CHURCH

No-one's been in a church since 1973 but that doesn't stop people wanting to get married in them. That's because they are cute and quaint and every girl dreams of walking down the aisle and everyone turning round and watching her in her gorgeous white satin dress. We can't help it, we're built that way. Men on the other hand, unless they are committed Christians, in which case they are unlikely to be getting married at all, don't give a stuff where they get married as long as it doesn't cost too much and their mother is happy with the arrangement, often mutually exclusive of course.

As you get older you do more sobbing at weddings, because you do more sobbing generally, so your child's wedding if you are a Grumpy Old Woman is going to leave you clutching wet sodden tissues, and if you are the bride's mother you are likely to start crying the moment you get to church, and then once the music starts your make-up will be a sodden mess throughout the service. When choosing a hat, it's worth bearing in mind to get one you can hide underneath when the sobbing starts. The only thing that will stop you sobbing if you are the bride's mother is when the teeny-weeny bridesmaid or 3-year-old page boy starts screaming during the important bits of the ceremony or decides to tell everyone he wants a wee and everyone starts laughing. This is your little girl's day and if there weren't so many people watching you would smack his legs.

THE SERVICE

Everyone's in a bloody panic, it feels like there is so much at stake, everything has to be perfect and when it's not – i.e. when it rains or the car turns up late, or the photographer is very, very annoying or when the florist delivers someone else's bouquet – it all feels very, very important indeed. Truth is the best weddings are really rather laid-back affairs. Having said that, I've never actually been to one.

Once you get into church the reality of the legal agreement kicks in. It's that bit where the vicar says something along the lines of, 'We are gathered here to join together two people in matrimony before God.' It's that 'before' God' bit that feels so very, very grown up, so very, very final. Then there's that other dramatic bit when the vicar says, 'If anyone knows any reason why these two should not be joined in holy matrimony' and everyone wants the ex to burst through the door like Dustin Hoffman in *The Graduate* yelling 'Elaine' and wielding a six-foot crucifix. Bride and bridegroom are so nervous they can only be trusted with saying one or two words at a time – because they are so befuddled with the stress of it all they might forget their own names or the name of the person they are marrying. It's really all rather comical.

THE RECEPTION

The idea of the reception is fabulous since everyone is dying for a drink, and almost everyone is looking forward to tucking into a serious amount of food since they have all been watching their weight for a year and the bride and bridesmaids and the bride's mother haven't eaten at all for a month for fear of not fitting into their frocks. So there is a collective sigh of relief all round, which inevitably results in immediate drunkenness and over-emotional behaviour. It is a relief, unless of course you are the bride's parents and/or you are footing the bill ... or both.

But it's always such a bloody palaver, isn't it? Uncle Arnold is going to make a pratt of himself again, feel up the bride's sister and get himself punched by her builder's labourer boyfriend. The speeches are going to go on for ever – and the best man is guaranteed to go way too far. Frankly, you don't want to hear about what the groom was doing to your daughter on their first night together – as far as you were concerned, she was still a virgin.

THE SPEECHES

There are some simple rules when it comes to speeches at weddings:

Say something nice about the bride, the bridesmaids and the
    bride's mother – even if none of it is true
Do not be afraid of the cliché – you are expected to say that the
    bride looks like an English rose or takes your breath away.
    Do not under any circumstances make any jokes about how
    the bride or bridesmaids look. You will end up in casualty
Avoid trying to be funny; unless you are Jack Dee or Victoria
    Wood, stand-up is best left to the professionals
Never, ever use a book full of suggested jokes and speeches; it
    will only make you look sad and tragic and ruin your
    chances with either of the fabulous bridesmaids

THE PHOTOS

Why do they take so long? Why are they such a pain in the neck? And why are they so expensive? OK, so everyone wants the odd nice photo, but posing for photos regularly ruins people's wedding day. Worse still, most people these days also have the wedding video too, which means that there are two people anxious to position you and get you to smile, or look down, or look winsome. Hours and hours of trying to get the right people in the right group and really it is such a colossal waste of time.

It's also got a whole lot worse. With families being infinitely more fragmented than ever before, the wedding photos become a punch-up if you are not careful ... 'Now can we have the bride's parents' is all very well, except that they divorced and have new partners and are barely speaking. And Auntie Florrie in the purple coat and fox-fur is getting her mug in front of everyone in every shot and the bride is five months pregnant.

Wedding photos are traditionally displayed on the mantelpiece in a silver frame. Both of you will look soppy and gormless and too young to know what you are doing. You were! Let's face it, he was so soppy and gormless he needed help tying his shoelaces on the day. The rest of the photos will have been pasted into a special photo album, possibly white leatherette with embossed silver wedding bells on the front. Yes – weddings have always been a bit naff. As you flip through your wedding album with its crinkled tissue leaves, certain things will strike you: for starters, just how peculiar hairdos were back then and how many people you used to know are now dead.

THE HONEYMOON

Yours was in Bognor or, at a pinch, maybe Amsterdam. Once again, these days they have got vastly more ambitious and more expensive. Your own children will be much more likely to splash out on three weeks in Bali and stopping off in Vegas on the way home.

IT'S THEIR CHOICE – NOT YOURS

This is the shocking truth when it comes to your children picking their partners for life. They may be years beyond the legal age of consent but do they really have to say 'yes' to such a loser?

Trouble is the mistakes you made at your own wedding are bound to be repeated when your own offspring get married because, if there's one sure thing, it is that they will not listen to you about the mistakes you made or experiences you have had in your own life. Don't be silly. And obviously no future partner is ever going to be good enough. That's a given.

God it's hard not to interfere, particularly for us mothers. Men tend to opt out of interfering in case they get the blame when everything goes wrong. Mums don't care. They knew it was all going to go wrong in the first place. The words, 'I told you so' are constantly hovering about their lips.

Some 'mistakes' your daughter might want to marry:

A poet. He will never ever earn enough money to feed a family; even the Poet Laureate is on about sixteen grand a year *

A footballer. God forbid. After all that money you've spent on her education, this is a man who is going to have trouble signing his own name on the registers

A pop star. Oh dear. If he's one of those druggie ones he'll be spending the honeymoon in rehab. Mind you, the great thing about pop stars is that they tend to have very innocuous parents – just the sort of couple you wouldn't mind going on a caravan holiday with

Someone in IT. She doesn't know what it means, you don't know what it means, he tried to explain but it was very dull

The bloke next door. Hoorah, your wishes have come true, baby is coming home; well not quite home, but next door. Maybe

* From the Department of Unreliable Information

you can drill a hole between the two houses and come and
go as you please; she might not be happy ever after, but
you're thrilled

Seriously, this list could be endless. You will never quite trust him,
whoever he is. He could be a barrister or a policeman and you will
still think he's shifty, she could work for a children's charity saving
street kids in Brazil, but you'd still think she was a bit of a show-off.
We are simply not programmed to welcome the strangers who
come to steal our children – unless of course your kids are such a
pain in the neck that you can't wait to get rid of them, in which
case, any Tom, Dick, Harry, Lizzie, Hannah or Kim will do.

Daughters-in-law from hell include:

Anorexic dancer. It would be fine if she was with the Royal
Ballet, but this one's just done *Footloose* in Bulgaria
A foreign girl. She will take him back to her foreign homeland
and you will never see your grandchildren – not fair
Career woman. She's older; even if she's not she looks it. She
won't look after him properly, she'll be too busy doing
spreadsheets on her computer to make shepherd's pie and
she'll probably end up sleeping with her boss just to 'get on'
– ooh, she's hard
A vegetarian. Well it might be alright for her, but your boy has
always liked his meat. As for coming over for Sunday lunch,
don't expect nut roasts and spinach felafel. If you're really
hungry, there's a tin of tuna in the cupboard. It's the
children I feel sorry for (not that they've got any – she's
probably too anaemic)

There's a sod's law about in-laws. If you're a highly articulate, book-
reading, cinema-going media couple, your in-laws will, by sod's
law, turn out to be cider-swigging, bingo-mad thickos, who don't

give a stuff about apostrophes. It's as if your kids have got together in order to play some elaborate practical joke.

Of course there is always the chance that you will get on famously and start playing badminton together. Inevitably, if this is the case, the 'kids' will split up and the four of you will be more upset than they are.

Of course there is something worse than having a wedding to pay for and that is not having a wedding to pay for. The thought of our children being left on the shelf is unbearable. What I say is bring on arranged marriages. Now that's what I call having complete control. Forget being in charge of choosing the buttonholes; button-holing a bride or a groom – now that's more like it.

What we're looking for ideally in a son-in-law:

Lives 17.5 miles away (not close enough to be 'just dropping by'–
      but near enough for regular visits)
Good cook – don't see why Sunday lunch should always be at ours
Chatty – if not naturally, then at least prepared to make the effort
Puts napkin in lap – not tucked into neck
Not too stuck up to wear a paper hat on Xmas Day
Someone who can change a carburettor or at least fix a new plug
      on a set of electric rollers

What we're looking for in a daughter-in-law:

Another witch to join the coven – sorry, I mean a nice friendly
      girl who doesn't sulk
Food allergy free; i.e., wheat and dairy tolerant
Chatty but not one of those silly cows who can't stop talking
Someone who will alert us when there is a good sale on in Hobbs
Someone who doesn't say, 'Whatever's easiest' when you offer to
      make them a cup of tea or coffee

Truth is you're not at all sure about the potential son- or daughter-in-law. If it's a son-in-law, no-one was ever going to be good enough for your special little girl; and, even though she's now twenty-five and earning more than you are, you still think of her as about ten. If his surname had been Gates and he'd been the more talented middle brother between Bill and Gareth, he still wouldn't have measured up. As it is, he's a labourer from Poland who seems to spend most of his time digging out people's cellars – and you're just hoping that it's with their knowledge.

Or if it's a daughter-in-law then Mum is pretty sure that both of them are going to get the shock of their lives when your son realises that she's unlikely to iron his pyjamas or make his eggy-bread just the way he's been used to for all these years.

Either way, whether you are marrying off a daughter or a son, these days you are probably going to have to pay for some or all of it. Back in the day when you got married it cost what was then thought an extortionate £2k. These days you can add a zero on the end.

Weddings are officially ridiculously, obscenely expensive and at every turn you are going to feel that you are being mean and horrid objecting to any of it. What is the divorce rate again? Are you sure it is going to be for life?

No wonder fewer people are getting married than ever before … According to figures from the Office of National Statistics, there were 132,562 divorces in 2006 in England and Wales, which is down 7% on 2005, so the lowest number in thirty years. But don't be deceived; fewer people are getting married in the first place. In 2005, for instance, the number of marriages was at its lowest level since records began in 1862.

Maybe the answer is to be foot-loose and fancy-free – since there is a lot of it about … One in three 25–34 -year-olds is now alone, and a quarter of late thirty somethings. It's also estimated that 23% of all 45–54 -year-olds are single or divorced. Time to get a cat.

6 · Resignation: the rot sets in

This chapter covers the stage when you realise that your relationship is as good as it's ever going to get and that the two of you are now destined for his and hers winged-back (vinyl) chairs, matching commodes and trying to get frisky on the stairlift. It's not that you are in this phase just yet, because once you are you will probably be too gaga to notice or too immobile to do anything about it, and in any case there's no point getting all huffy about it and trying to do any better because by then no-one else will have you.

MARRIAGE: THE ROT SETS IN

OK, so love is magical for about three years, on and off, and you get some nice wedding presents and some nice photos of you (looking slim) and the world treats your relationship with respect and (misplaced) admiration, and hey you might get some fabulous children, but the day-in, day-out slog of it all is frankly a bit of a pain in the neck. Sooner or later his habit of walking out of a closed door and leaving it open rather than closing it behind him, or her obsession with towel folding or lousy gravy-making will start to get you down. The trouble is it's so hard to just – well – walk away. It's not that you dislike him, well not constantly at least, and it's not that your marriage or partnership is a pile of poo; if it was, you would walk out. But it takes some working at that's for sure and eventually, when they go away to the annual sales conference, you have to admit you look forward to having the kitchen and the bathroom and the remote – oh, and the bed – to yourself for a few days.

Why does marriage have to be so, tangibly and publicly permanent? Why can't we have a virtual marriage, or a virtual partnership to use that ugly word? What about a buy one get one free, or a pool of partners to chose from on a weekly or monthly basis? What about making it a legal requirement of staying married for your partner to change according to your prioritised demands? For instance, why can't there be laws against men who don't know the difference between 'in the bin' and 'the side of the bin', or who borrow the fuse from your hairdryer without telling you (so that you think it's broken and go out and spend eighteen quid on a new one) or laws against women who 'accidentally' take your favourite anorak to the charity shop or scrape the car whilst reversing out of a one-way street and fail to own up? None of us is perfect, we've all got our little foibles. Let's face it, one man's 'little habit' can be one woman's 'last straw'.

Every relationship has its rocky patches. You can't just bale out, not without a fight. Arguing is as much a part of living together as sex, sometimes more. We can sulk, we can slam doors, we can be as difficult as we please: truth is we have to kiss and make up and get on with it.

ARGUMENTS

Men and women argue in different ways, which makes the argument an argument in the first place. Men cite logic, and then claim to have won the argument because the woman is being illogical, or that she won't see logic, and women lash out and say things that are unbelievably spiteful ... And are, well, not very logical. Unfortunately, once a man tells a woman that she is being illogical, it just fuels her hysteria and anger some more, so the more he tells her she is being illogical the more illogical she will be.

Either that or one partner goes from 0 to 100 miles an hour argument-wise in three seconds and the other refuses to get into argument gear at all, and of course the less the person you are arguing with argues back the more you want to argue. There is nothing worse than someone who refuses to enter the argument fray because all you do is get redder in the face and more and more angry and resort to ever more spiteful remarks. The more silent they become the more moral high ground they retain. Which is after all very maddening indeed.

How to start an argument

The best place to start an argument is somewhere that you can bang things about, somewhere say like the kitchen where you can thwack saucepans down on the work surface or slam cupboard doors. It's best to do this sort of thing in a martyr-like display – much better to scrub the saucepans and slap them down on the draining board, rather than just bang them down per se; that way you retain the moral high ground (up to a point) and still make a hell of a din.

Something little can spark the argument off, like they left the shed door open all night, or have eaten the last of the Branston pickle, or they left you the car with no petrol in. Actually, I suppose all of those are quite big things really. The point is little things are big things when it comes to arguments. Everything – even the way they are arguing or are standing while they are arguing – is annoying and fuels the argument some more.

How to win or finish an argument

Normally arguments end with one person flouncing out of the room/house/car, or because someone has to leave for work or occasionally because one person falls asleep. If you are going to do any flouncing or storming off it is important not to do this when you would be left in a position where you will have to ring them about five minutes later for help. So telling them to stop the car and flouncing off on the hard shoulder, or storming off in the middle of a shopping centre when they've got your purse and the car keys is simply bad planning. And it will make you feel very silly. Worse, you will have to pretend you thought they were right all along in order to make them turn around and come and rescue you.

It is quite possible for two people to win an argument. In fact, in my experience both people do (think) they have won the argument. Which is probably just as well because otherwise the simmering and resentment would just go on for ever.

Things Grumpy Old Couples might want to argue over

Money

Sex

Things that have gone off in the fridge

Anything that's got blocked

Piles of stuff on the stairs that someone could break their neck
    tripping over

The butter knife in the marmalade/blackcurrant jam

Leaving lights on

Putting too much water in the kettle so that it takes half an hour
    to boil

Using expensive face wipes to remove scum from around the
    bath

Looking bored when you're meant to be having a conversation

Not passing on telephone messages

Being careless about olive pips getting lodged in the dishwasher

Money and sex ... again

THE POWER STRUGGLE

In any long-term relationship, many arguments boil down to the same problem, or the same argument: the ongoing power struggle, which is essentially who in the couple is in charge of what. On average, most couples spend the first twenty years jostling for position; after that one partner definitely takes over. And it's usually the woman. You can tell this because so many men over the age of fifty are sent out to the shops with frankly matronly shopping bags (any man holding a girlie or matronly shopping bag has thrown in the towel power-struggle-wise). Such men are seen at the shops with the list that she made for them, and they have been told to stick to the things on the list. Their partner might even have written next to the word tomatoes, 'nice', on the basis that he cannot be trusted to choose nice ones on his own.

For some reason the correct term for this type of man is hen-pecked. But he has just given in for an easier life. Poor man has got on with doing his little jobs and mowing the lawn (when asked) and tries to get out of the house as much as possible (hence fishing, golf, or just 'out of the house' but within reach of the loo which, as a man gets older and is more prone to prostate problems, is a plus). Women, being the illogical creatures that they are, rejoice at now being in charge but simultaneously lament living with a man who is now no longer masculine. So they chastise him for not taking charge or thinking for himself, or being a man, but on the other hand they like being the one who decides which colour the spare bedroom is painted.

Of course sometimes it's the man who is in control but this is much less fashionable than it used to be. Basically, ever since the seventies when women got really uppity, the female of the species is happier to opt for divorce rather than being told what shoes to wear.

There was a time when women were supposed to accessorise their husbands and be demure submissive types with properly arranged hair and un-laddered tights. This was back in the day when women weren't supposed to worry their pretty little heads about 'world issues' and knew nothing about politics. Of course the great thing about being a woman nowadays is that we still don't know anything about world issues and politics but that doesn't mean we can't talk about these things in very loud tones at dinner parties.

The television

Battles over the TV have been redrawn. There is usually more than one TV in the house – ah, but only one wide-screen flash one bought quite recently. This will be the one in the front room along with the sofa, drinks cabinet and toasty fire. Yes, there are other tellies dotted around the house; the kids have tellies in their bedrooms (even though you thought it was a silly idea) and there's always the black-and-white portable in the spare room with a coat hanger shoved down the back, which you can watch if you're desperate.

However many tellies you have, then, there is only one prime telly and it only has one remote control. And so this is the main battleground. Women are drawn to the fridge or the phone, which makes them vulnerable to domination by remote (i.e someone else controlling the buttons), so, short of having a rota, many couples resort to dividing the time in front of the TV into slots. Policing it could be tricky, although I imagine most children would throw themselves into the role with enthusiasm, especially if they are subjected to a bossy form teacher at school.

Personally I think the black-and-white in the spare room is starting to look more and more attractive, plus getting up every five minutes to wiggle the coat-hanger around is really good exercise.

Things women like to control in the home

What we are going to have for supper – hence, if she is on a diet,
 so are you

The shopping list. Anything she forgets to put on the list will
 be your fault, because you could at least have 'thought'. She
 will accuse you of 'not thinking' even if you didn't even go to
 the supermarket, even if you were seventeen miles away at
 the time

Whether supper is going to be 'on trays on our knees' or 'sitting
 up at the table'

Choice of lavatory paper – white/luxury possibly a blue or a pink
 in the downstairs cloakroom (depending on decor).
 Remember anything silly, cheap or a 'funny yellow' is not on

The social diary: who is coming for supper and when. It's important no social engagement is accepted or offered without
 running it past the boss first – she may want to watch a bit-
 tersweet comedy drama on the telly that night and anyway
 she's never liked Brian and Sue. Gradually you will realise
 that over the years it's her friends who get invited round for
 dinner (proper dinner complete with smelly cheeses and
 port) whilst your friends are relegated to swift halves in the
 pub

Leaving notes for the cleaner/gardener; you may leave money,
 but instructions are her territory

The number of decorative cushions on the bed

Things women prefer men to be in control of in the home

Paying the bills

Walking down to the local shop to buy brown sauce when she's
 forgotten to pick some up in the supermarket

Any small DIY jobs, such as bleeding of radiators and touching-
 up of chipped paint

Garden/shed/car stuff
Guttering and slates on the roof
The boiler
The bulk buying of wine, bottled water, mixers and spirits –
    an all year round duty but particularly crucial at Xmas

SEX AFTER MARRIAGE

Sex after marriage dwindles in regularity as we all know. After all, where's the fun if there is nothing at all to stop you, plus the kids come along and now there is everything to stop you. The net result is that marriage is not the hotbed of sex it's cracked up to be ...

All that women's magazine stuff – you'll have to make time, make 'me' time. Oh shut up, just do it when you can. Knock it out, it's just another job to tick off the list, isn't it really?   ARABELLA WEIR

Sex – or no sex – around Britain

In Scotland 10% of women regard sex as a household chore
There are more vibrators sold in the UK every year than washing
    machines and tumble driers combined. How amazing is
    that? Not as amazing as it would be if they invented a
    vibrator that would also do the washing. (As Grumpy Old
    Women, may we just say we have no problem with the use
    of sex toys as long as said sex toys are rinsed thoroughly in
    a Dettol-based solution after every use.)
People in the Midlands are most likely to experiment sexually –
    for instance 40% have tried handcuffs
In the southwest 45% of those questioned said they had little
    or no sex at all – but then think of all the pebble-dash
    bungalows
The Welsh proved the most passionate with 48% of people

saying they had sex at least once a week, so those Male Voice
Choirs might be a good place to pull

Wales also had the lowest number of women faking their
orgasms: 4.8% against a national average of 7.6%

People in Yorkshire have the most sex per year of everyone
(128 times) but that's possibly because they're too mean to
put the central heating on. The Northern Irish the least
(102 times)

43% of all Brits have had sex in a park

18% of Londoners are likely to have had sex at work – saucy
devils. Anything other than face the commute home. Let's
face it, if you spend an extra forty minutes having nookie in
the stationery cupboard, chances are that the rush hour will
be over by the time you get to the station and you'll get a seat
all the way back to Ongar.

(All from national relationship survey, Tickbox for Zestra UK,
August 2006)

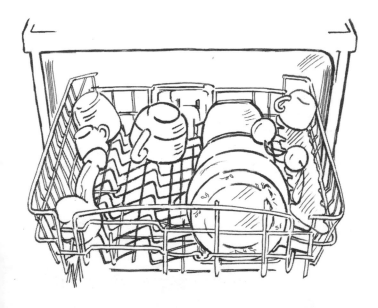

CHILDREN

It's a miracle that anyone manages to have kids at all given how much less frequent sex is once you get married or been in a relationship for a while. But they do. Once the children come along, of course you are glued together good and proper as a couple (and so you should be) but on a practical level children put yet another strain on your relationship. The formula for the effect children have on a relationship goes something like this:

Sleep deprivation + the in-laws coming round more often than usual + stretch marks = a sudden drop in desire + increasing resentment at being the one who either goes out to work and earns the bacon, or resentment because you are the one left at home changing nappies and trying to get the buggy in and out of the car boot four times a day. Either way, naturally, each half of the partnership feels the most hard done by.

Once the kids come along you can multiply the household tasks by about a squillion. Suddenly having the bedspreads dry-cleaned or the silver polished recedes so far into the background noise as to be irrelevant. With newborn babies it is a matter of trying to get a meal on a plate (rather than on a table), a bath run and finishing off a poo properly without being interrupted. Then factor in the lack of sleep, and the lack of sex, and you have a mighty boil of resentment which bursts at the slightest provocation – like when she chucks his vinyl collection into the garage, smashing half of it, or she turns the living room into one massive changing mat/playroom. Adult needs go, children's needs come in big time. The best relationships recover, but many don't.

SEX AND BABIES

So why do women go off sex when they are pregnant?

They've finally got what they wanted

They think it will dent the baby's head. It doesn't matter how
      many textbooks you read denying this myth, there is always
      going to be doubt. No-one wants to sabotage their child's
      chance of studying classics at Oxford

Sex after birth

Men sometimes go off sex having witnessed the messy end during
the birth. For some men it's a bit like having fought in Vietnam;
there are hideous flashbacks to deal with. If a man is squeamish
it's best not to 'look down there' whilst attending the birth. Once the
baby's born, women can be quite tender down there, and the only
thing they can contemplate around their nether regions is a bag
of frozen peas.

There is something off-putting about having nookie when the
baby is slumbering next to you in a pristine Moses basket. Doesn't
seem right. Ditto when the baby is older and will only sleep in your
bed: this is one of the best forms of contraception known to man.
It's a miracle any siblings are ever born.

However, siblings do get born and the pressure mounts up.
How couples manage to have sex at all when the children are little
and are constantly wetting the bed or puking up or having night-
mares or needing a glass of water is a mystery. I know a couple
who used to sneak off to the tree house and pull the rope ladder
up behind them.

CHILDREN OR DOGS

For many couples, witnessing their friends procreate is enough to
put them off for life, which is why lots of people choose dogs
instead.

Reasons to have dogs rather than kids:

Dogs don't fall off the top of the slide, bite their own tongue

and go all limp, necessitating a horrendously scary dash
to the A&E

Dogs don't demonstrate a worrying lack of co-ordination by
scribbling over the lines in a colouring-in book

Dogs don't get letters sent home from school about pinching
little girls in the playground

Dogs can't skin up joints and drink cider when they are meant
to be at Katie's house doing their geography homework

Dogs don't have a Facebook or MySpace account randomly
asking strangers to come to a party and trash the house
whilst the parents are attending a funeral at the other end
of the country

Dogs don't fail their GCSEs

Dogs don't go on holiday with their parents and look miserable
for the duration because they're not with their stupid mates

Dogs don't need mobile phones or ridiculous trainers or green
nail varnish

Dogs don't fail their GCSE retakes

Dogs don't have their tongues pierced

EMPTY NESTS

Of course we curse the kids, their mess, the noise, the constant
trips to Center Parcs and kiddie-friendly restaurants, all those vile
lunches in pubs with plastic playground equipment, the unpractised
pianos, those pointless fencing lessons, the redundant cello, and
most galling of all – the bare-faced ingratitude. But the fact is, it
doesn't go on for ever. Children grow up and unless something
goes a bit wrong, they leave home.

At this point the Grumpy Old Couple will be faced with the
empty nest. Emotions will be mixed. There might be bottles of
champagne opened and jigs of joy on the front lawn or the two
of you could take to your beds and sob for a month. For most

couples the reaction to the kids leaving home will be a mixture of highs and lows. Highs because you can get a decent night's sleep instead of sitting bolt upright at 3 a.m., not sure if it's one of yours coming home or a burglar, and lows because, although it's nice to have some quiet, it's a bit too quiet. This is when you do weird stuff like sniff their pillows and get sentimental about their old pencil case.

On the one hand a whole new chapter of your life is opening up but you're not sure you like the way the book is heading. Hmmm.

Big decisions tend to be made around this time. Some people decide they should move house and maybe a bungalow would be a good idea. A bungalow might be a good idea though occasionally you will forget you have moved into a bungalow and drive yourself mad trying to find the stairs.

Downsizing in general is a neat solution to preventing your grown-up offspring from returning to the roost. There is a worrying number of what they call 'the boomerang generation', who move out only to wing their way back to Mummy and Daddy once their university days are over. It must be very galling to downsize only to have your children return home, especially if you have more kids than bedrooms. After all, it's very tricky to have a nice game of bridge with the neighbours when you've got a big hairy 26-year-old who has taken up residence on your sofa and won't stop farting.

The alternative is to stay in the old house and fill it with hobby paraphernalia such as mountaineering stuff or Chinese orphans. Most women will have a last surge of broodiness in their late forties. This is when they start talking about adoption, especially after a couple of glasses of Pinot Grigio. As a man it's probably best to humour her, even to go as far as getting some brochures or looking up 'Chinese orphanages' on the internet. You know what she's like. If you say, 'No', she'll go ahead and do it. Just quietly indulge her and she'll go off the idea in her own time.

Broody middle-aged women who are no longer able to procreate and can't quite be bothered to go through with the whole adoption thing will succumb to odd syndromes such as 'grandmother envy' and might start doing strange things like buying booties in Mothercare for fictitious grandkiddies. This should probably be nipped in the bud, but compared to the real atrocities that are going on around the world it's pretty harmless.

Of course the other problem with not downsizing when you've got that window of opportunity is that, once the kids have moved out, his mother/your mother – whichever's worse – will move in.

Just remember there isn't a kitchen in the world that is big enough for two women. The only way that having a nanna moving in works is if you've got enough space for a self-contained granny flat and she's still fit enough to do a bit of weeding.

Much more sensible than having 'mother' move in is to get yourselves a lodger. The lodger will pay rent, he might also be quite nice looking, in which case you'd better buy some new pants because you don't want him pegging out his smalls next to your massive great raggedy bloomers.

Of course the lodger may well be female, in which case make sure she's quite plain, otherwise the old man will start holding in his tummy and rearranging his parting – the silly old fool.

Things you can do with their room when the kids have gone

Convert it into a darkroom/artist's studio/hobby and craft room.
    At last you've got somewhere private to indulge your secret
    doll's house fetish
Install a sauna/table tennis table
Breed guinea pigs in there
Turn it into a sex dungeon

A sex tip for the grumpy couple
Do it regularly. Every birthday. Even if you don't feel like it.

GRUMPY PILLOW TALK (OR SEX IN THE GRUMPY MARRIAGE)

It's so long since I've had sex that I've forgotten who ties up whom. JOAN RIVERS

The difference between sex and death is that with death you can do it alone and no-one is going to make fun of you. WOODY ALLEN

I don't see much of Alfred since he got so interested in sex. MRS ALFRED KINSEY

Sex at age ninety is like trying to shoot pool with a rope. GEORGE BURNS

As I grow older and older and totter toward the tomb, I find I care less and less who goes to bed with whom. DOROTHY L. SAYERS

I can still enjoy sex at 74. I live at 75, so it's no distance. BOB MONKHOUSE

I'm at the age where food has taken the place of sex in my life. In fact I've just had a mirror put over my kitchen table. RODNEY DANGERFIELD

Of course no-one thinks anyone over fifty does it at all – no-one under thirty anyhow. Sex and older people is something of a taboo. The reason why young people don't think old people have sex is that you don't see older people being portrayed as sexy in the media. If every other day the *Sun*'s page 3 stunna was over fifty then everyone would get used to the idea ... maybe ... Or maybe sales of the *Sun* would simply plummet?

THE SEVEN-YEAR ITCH

According to MORI, peak discontentment occurs between six and nine years of marriage, give or take a year or two. But what's a couple of years between friends? A MORI survey of 1,000 married couples showed that one in five wives wakes up sometimes and wishes she wasn't married any more, compared to one in seven husbands. These figures doubled if the woman had children or was working ... And presumably quadrupled once the couple was in late middle age.

> *I think we should be teaching relationship skills in schools – how to survive day to day, what to do if you're bored silly, what to do if you're in a rut. All these things are relationship skills and it really annoys me that people think you don't need to work at it: you have to work bloody hard actually.*   TRACEY COX

So perhaps it is time to remind ourselves of those wedding vows:

I, (...), take you (...), to be my wife, to have and to hold from this day forward; for better, for worse, for richer, for poorer, in sickness and in health, to love and to cherish, (or to love, cherish and worship) till death us do part, according to God's holy law; and this is my solemn vow.

The thing about marriage is that the longer you are together the more your wedding vows will be tested. As we get older we are more likely to start falling to pieces. It happens with everything –

washing machines, dishwashers, men and women – so let's start with 'for better, for worse'.

Well, we all have our ups and downs, but when the downs out-number the ups then you're in trouble. What no-one should have to deal with is a sudden out-of-the-blue dramatic tilt to the bad, which is why you should never marry an actor.

I know an actor who was regularly earning over £150,000 a year, then, all of a sudden, the bottom dropped out of his appeal and instead of raking in the £150,000 like normal he earned just £8,000 – now that's a lot worse than £150k. What was his poor wife supposed to do? Stand by him, bolster his squashed ego, remove the bottle/gun from his hand?

Yes, that's what she should have done, but instead she panicked and left him for an accountant. Three years later, the actor got a job on an American soap and started making cubic money again. His ex-wife is still living in a three-bedroom semi in Swindon with the accountant. Let this be a lesson to us all.

I thought you were a millionaire
I thought you were a virgin

Which leads us neatly to 'for richer, for poorer'. Ideally the fortunes of a married couple should swing the other way. It's no big deal being young and skint and living on baked potatoes and sex, but when you're fifty you don't want to be poorer than you were when you first got wed. No-one wants to spend their middle years living in a skip, eating cat food. Thing is, bad stuff happens and the trouble with hitting your fifties is that the dreaded redundancy bug can strike at any time.

Some men are so scared of telling their wives that they've lost their job that they don't; they pretend to go to work every day and spend eight hours in amusement arcades and cafés before daring to go home. This is bad. This is the stuff of nervous breakdowns, which leads us neatly to 'in sickness and in health'.

IN SICKNESS AND IN HEALTH – HOW TO BEHAVE WHEN YOUR PARTNER IS POORLY

There is nothing worse than a sick man apart from a sick woman. This is because when a woman says she's not feeling herself it's probably something quite serious like fibroids, which after a series of scans will eventually require a small operation after which your lady will need plenty of recuperation time and will not 'be able to lift a thing'.

When men are ill on the other hand it tends to be something quite inconsequential, like constipation or indigestion, and nothing that can't be sorted out by some figs. Of course it's a well-known fact that men tend to collapse into bed at the first sniffle, which is actually preferable to the female habit of playing the martyr in the dressing gown, pulling herself around the house dragging the Hoover behind her, 'Because if I don't do it, then nobody will', which is true of course but really, what I say is: if you've got pleurisy woman, let the airing cupboard go to rack and ruin for a few days; it'll be so much more fun tackling it when you're better.

I (Jenny) was brought up by a Northern mother who didn't believe in illness. Both your legs would have to be hanging off before she would deem you unfit to ride a bicycle to school. All of us three kids ended up having emergency appendix operations because she didn't believe we didn't have 'tummy ache' from 'eating too many sweets'.

There's probably a fine line between wuss and martyr. The fact is us women don't like our men to be ill; not unless they've got something like a bullet wound or they fell out of a helicopter. There is nothing unsexier than the adult male in pyjamas during daylight hours – especially if the top is tucked into the bottoms and said male is clutching a mug of Lemsip – yuk.

The trouble is more things are likely to go wrong as we get older – and weird things too. For example, my partner got a bone-eating fungus in his cheek. Yes, it was dreadful. I was run off my feet for weeks and in the end he had to go into hospital. What a relief. The night he was under the knife was the first decent night's sleep I'd had in six months.

What's particularly boring is when men break a leg doing something stupid like go-karting for a mate's fiftieth. You are fifty years old, so what are you doing go-karting? There is always a bit of spite in a wife's vengeful brain that wishes he'd broken both legs, because that would have taught him a real lesson.

Men: some other 'accidents' that will elicit zero sympathy from your Grumpy Old Woman

Falling out of a tree
Not looking where you are going and bumping into a lamp
    post
Hitting self on head with own golf club
Tripping over shoelace
Running out between two parked cars to get an ice cream when
    you are older than nine years old

Ditto head stuck between bannister rails
Concussion as a result of small electrical job going wrong
Dropping something very heavy on foot
Getting something in your eye when you should have been
      wearing goggles in the first place
Getting something stuck in your ear; why would you put the
      nozzle of your bicycle wheel in your ear in the first place

Fact

Men like having slings. When they look in the mirror they can
pretend they've been fighting in the Crimean war.

Rule of nursing thumb

Personally I think that domestic nursing should operate on a
sliding scale of guilt. If the injury is entirely his fault, then he
should get three Cuppa Soups a day and the remote control for
the television should be positioned just beyond his reach. Other
subtle punishments include not helping him sweep toast
crumbs out of the bed, or 'forgetting' to change his limp soup-
stained sheets. If the fact that he's in bed for three weeks isn't really
his fault – for example he caught Legionnaires' disease trying to
keep you in cashmere jumpers – then the least he deserves is a bit
of sympathy: three nice meals on a tray, some sporting magazines
and a cool hand on his fevered brow. Finally, if it's your fault that
he's going to be in traction for six months – say you pushed him
down the stairs – then he should get silver service and choice of
pudding. Oh – and a medicinal blow job twice a week.

Fact

No woman looks good with an elastic bandage around her ankle. It
is a look that not even Kate Moss can pull off. The trouble with any
kind of injury that needs either a plaster cast or a bandage is that on
a woman over forty-five it looks like the accident might have been
drink related. Unfair but true.

LETTING YOURSELF GO

The rules on letting yourself go in a relationship are simple. You can't – unless they do. And then you can let go together and get fat in elasticated waistbands and slob out in front of the telly to your heart's content.

> *It's when you start buying your husband's underwear, it's when you are picking your toe-nails and she's plucking her moustache as you're watching* EastEnders. *I think that's probably when the romance has gone.*   JEFF GREEN

Truth is that couples who stay together for a long time become like one another. They start to morph into one another: she gets a moustache and hairy nostrils, and he gets man boobs and gets fussy about who moved his stapler. Thinness or fatness is a tricky area – because if one of you allows yourself to get a bit podgy and the other doesn't then this can often end in tears. But sometimes it is as simple as one of you staying thin, the other one thinks they have to stay thin, one of you gets fat and the other one thinks to hell with it I am going to get fat. Similarly, one of you gets into line-dancing big time and the other thinks if you can't beat them join them.

Of course, if you don't want to get fat (your partner might have a fast metabolism and be naturally thin) and look like Jack Spratt's wife, here's a handy slimming tip. The best way to never put on weight is to starve yourself down to a size 10 tight-fitting pair of jeans and never ever take them off. OK, removal for bathing, lavatory and sexual purposes is acceptable, but it's advisable – once your nookie session is over – if you can't trust yourself not to go midnight snacking, to wear them in bed. Nothing reminds one more of the curse of the calorie than the denim dig, that unforgiving feeling of being strangled around the gut by your own jeans.

Pants and socks

For some reason when a woman gets married she takes on the role of pants and sock buyer. She will do this for her husband and children until they get married and the old man dies. It is a very modern and rare man who will think, 'I must nip to Marks and buy the family some socks in my lunch hour.'

The fact that we are responsible for everyone's underwear for so long means that we end up putting ourselves last, which is why so many middle-aged women will have an underwear crisis. Most of us don't realise what a state we have allowed our pants and bras to get into until one day we hang them out on the washing-line and the new handsome next-door neighbour leans over the fence for a chat, catches sight of your knackered old undies and turns a bit green. Oh, the shame.

The problem with being forty-plus is that we feel we owe it to ourselves to be comfortable and being comfortable rules out thongs. There are very few women over twenty-five that can wear a thong without one's buttock cheeks looking like massive spam panniers garrotted by a length of dental floss. We like 'apple catchers': nice big comfy pants that have plenty of room to tuck a hanky into.

ROMANCE – HOW TO KEEP IT GOING IN A GRUMPY RELATIONSHIP

Go for separate everything: tellies, beds, bank accounts ...

Do not succumb to en-suite madness. It's all very well for Kirstie and Phil to extol the virtues on *Location, Location, Location* but the reality is that you are lying in bed with your fingers in your ears while he evacuates his bowels on the dot of 6 a.m. I wouldn't mind but he doesn't finish till seven. Ooh, they don't half take their time in there – and to be honest Sainsbury's whiff of Alpine Meadow plug-in air freshener doesn't stand a chance. The en-suite stinks of poo and nothing but poo for at least forty-five minutes, during which you've got to clean your teeth without collapsing into a dead faint.

> *I think there are some things in a relationship that are best just left, and I would say poo for me quite significantly falls into that category. And there's nothing worse than lying in bed in the morning if you have an en-suite bathroom and opening your eyes and your nostrils to the smell of your beloved's huge morning poo.*
> TANYA BYRON

Personally we think men and women should have his and her bathrooms and preferably his should be down the bottom of the garden. Here are some other things you can spend your money on rather than an en-suite bathroom:

A trip on the Orient Express
A quarter of a new kitchen
Some decking and possibly a water feature (by which we don't
    mean outdoor hot tub; where do you think you are – San
    Francisco?)

HOW TO PLEASE THE OTHER HALF

It's important to try and remember to flirt with each other now and again. Obviously you must discuss this in advance, otherwise he will be very scared when you suddenly start winking at him over the breakfast table. Remember flirting can backfire. I once sat on my partner's knee and by the time I got off it had gone numb, so much so that when he tried to stand up he fell over. There is nothing sexy about a man falling over just because you sat on his knee for five minutes.

He shouldn't try to carry you either – not if he's not sure he won't drop you. There's nothing more humiliating for a woman than her chap scooping her up in his arms only to say, 'Jesus woman I think I've slipped a disc.'

Also beware mucking about near water. It's all very well for young men and women to chase each other around the banks of a duck pond, but men tend to get clumsy as they get older and you will never be sure that he didn't push you in on purpose. This is the sort of thing that can refuel an argument – 'and you pushed me in the duck pond'.

When men get older they tend to develop a sweet tooth and take a lot of solace in sweeties. Most men over fifty like to have a toffee about their person at all times. For this reason we are going to include Jenny's dad's favourite joke:

> Old bloke goes into a sweet shop, proper old-fashioned sweet shop, full of jars of every kind of sweet you can think of. Behind the counter is a beautiful 19-year-old girl and a sign saying, 'Condoms fitted by hand'. 'Ah', says the old bloke, 'Who fits the condoms by hand?' 'I do,' says the beauty. 'In that case,' says the old man, 'go and wash your hands. I want a quarter of Liquorice Allsorts.'

Because men revert back to the tastebuds of their youth it's quite easy to make your other half happy without spending more than a couple of quid. Obviously they still really want blow jobs but if you're not in the mood try this tasty mixture:

A quarter of jelly babies
A quarter of wine gums
A quarter of coconut mushrooms or – if he doesn't like coconut
   – Liquorice Allsorts
A quarter of boiled limes with squidgy chocolate inside

If you buy him proper sweets now and again he will realise that even though sometimes you think he's an idiot, you love him truly. My parents' relationship has weathered some storms but thanks to walnut whips on a Friday and Thornton's misshapes they have managed to pull through.

FINDING SOMETHING IN COMMON
Shared hobbies

Jigsaw puzzles
Gardening
Car booting
Going for walks
Cycling (using fold-up bikes that you can fit in the boot of the car so
    that you can go somewhere nice like the New Forest for a cycle)
Bridge

Some pastimes have been specifically invented to cater to the middle-aged grumpy couple who need a shared pastime other than carping at each other over the breakfast table:

Making your own wine/quince jelly
Caravanning
Allotments
Tantric sex (just joking)
Mooching. National Trust properties, garden centres and
    organic farmers' markets are all good for a 'mooch around'.
    Organic farmers' markets where you can get a hot organic
    sausage sandwich are a particularly good idea

Certain towns make good mooching pastures for Grumpy Old Couples. I'd suggest Ely, which has a cathedral and good tea rooms (go on, ask for a vanilla slice and two forks). Bath is also nice for a trip out, being the perfect mix of historical interest and good shopping and of course Edinburgh, which not only has a castle but a Harvey Nicks too.

Hobbies for him that cannot be shared

Fishing – women are officially too noisy to fish.

Remember

The couple who 'mooch' together, stay together.

COMMUNICATING: OLD BOYS AND OLD GIRLS

When people have lived together as so-called lovers for so long that they look like, talk like and walk like one another, presumably the whole thing operates on an entirely different system of values. I love the way women totally take over, physically and intellectually, tell their husbands what to wear, buy them their clothes, determine their social diary. No wonder they retreat to their sheds or their fishing or golf.

Women retreat to their friends. I suppose the truth is you've sort of said all you want to say by the time you've been married for ten years, then you have the kids around for twenty years to interrupt or disrupt what you want to say to one another, and by the time they leave home you have forgotten what it is you wanted to say to one another in the first place.

Routine is also important as a Grumpy Old Couple. Often you know what the other one is going to say, what they are going to order in a restaurant, or what they are likely to say when you ask to swap orders because what they ordered looks nicer than yours.

There is nothing wrong with routine. It makes life easier when you know each other's little foibles.

Things you know about him

He likes navy-blue V-necks and red-and-white spotted handkerchiefs
He likes a thick-cut marmalade
He doesn't like kiwi fruit
He's a size 10 shoe and a 15½ in collar

He's prone to fungal infections such as athlete's foot
He doesn't wear a vest
Now and again he needs an anti-dandruff shampoo
He likes Radio 4 in the morning
He doesn't like queuing at petrol stations
His glasses are usually on the brown chest
He prefers a shower to a bath
He likes to read books about battleships
He always sleeps on the right but dresses to the left
He's right-handed, long-sighted and can burn easily
He likes his tea weak and his coffee strong; sometimes he
    likes a hot Ribena
His favourite soup is tomato
He likes Bob Dylan
He doesn't like jewellery

Things he knows about you
Er ... where you live

TALKING – OR AS THE AMERICANS WOULD CALL IT – COMMUNICATING

Women talk more than men, men pretend to listen: that's how we communicate.

On the other hand when a woman says she is a 'good listener' it's because she's deaf.

She says/he hears
She says Would you mind picking up some milk on the way home?

He hears Oh God, I'm so exhausted. You never even think to help. Oh no, it's me that has to remember every last thing. I don't even like milk. It's you that likes milk on your stupid cornflakes, which have run out – not that I'm going to tell you. No, for once in your stupid life you can go without cornflakes. They're no good for you anyway. What's the point in me buying Fruit and Fibre. I tell you, if you don't end up with an impacted colon it'll be a miracle.

He says Yes, no problem.

He thinks Well I suppose I will if I have to; like I haven't got more important things to be doing with my day than just popping into a supermarket and queuing up for about eight hours to buy a carton of milk. Milk you say; what kind of milk? I suppose I'm meant to guess. Ah, this is one of those trick questions. You say milk, I buy skimmed. It's wrong. I buy full fat: it's wrong, wrong, wrong, wrong. You're always trying to catch me out. As for size: do you want a litre, half litre or one of those baby cartons?

What he does He buys a large carton of full-fat milk, a medium-sized carton of semi-skimmed milk and a small carton of skimmed milk.

She thinks He's gone mad, the idiot.

ONE HOUSE OR TWO?

It would be so easy to live with someone if you didn't share the same address. Clearly being partners or even going the whole hog and being married would be relatively easy if couples did not have to live in the same house. Surely this would quarter or even halve the divorce rate at a stroke.

Next door might be too close, but then again it would be nice and economical. However, in the same street – at opposite ends – would perhaps be ideal, to the point of – well – I have no idea why it's not done more often. OK, there are financial considerations, but I think it has legs as an idea. Different beds guarantee a good night's sleep, but are close enough to bunk up and sleep together if the mood takes you. You'll also be able to call on one another for boiled eggs and bed baths if you're poorly or if – let's say – you need someone to let in the gas man, but crucially far enough away and separate enough to mean that 80% of couples' common problems simply would not apply.

None of the following areas of tension and argument would cloud your horizon. Think of that. His mother comes to stay for a week, and she stays with him, at number 52; your mother comes to stay and she stays with you, where she's not constantly reminded how disappointed she is in your choice of husband. But sadly there is no getting away from the fact that she will still be able to see how flimsy and superficial your cleaning of the house is, and you won't be able to stop her rummaging through your drawers and seeing how messy your clutter is.

And the children; well, for one thing they are less likely to see domestic and marital friction on a daily basis and therefore, although they might miss out on seeing both parents all the time, I can't see this being a big disadvantage. In fact, every child I know would see this as a big advantage. You could still chum up for big family meals and celebrations, and at the weekends the kids could alternate one weekend at his and one at hers. As long as they weren't far away and you didn't have to drive for an hour to collect their music practice or tennis racket, then it would be like being really happily divorced without all the bitterness and recrimination.

Cynics, romantics and the young will think this is an entirely negative arrangement and will worry about its sexual implications. However, unless you are in the first flush of sexual relationship excitement (two years max) this is not a problem, since you won't even notice not having sex on tap, let alone miss it. Anyway, if you are in the first flush of sexual excitement you are very unlikely to have bought or be reading this book.

If two homes is impractical
Make sure you claim some space in the shared marital abode that is unquestionably yours. For a man this is normally a comfy chair next to a table with a secret drawer full of nuts and caramel sweeties.

For women it might be a corner of the sofa where you stash your ladies' magazines, reading glasses and packet of emergency Garibaldi. The family should respect these places and treat them as no-go areas.

SPORT

On the whole, sport is to women what shoes are to men: an astonishingly baffling obsession that takes up too much time and money. OK, a bit of sport and a few pairs of shoes are understandable, but men go way over the top. They spend whole days in front of the rugby and cricket and watching everything on Sky Sports. That said, Sky Sports' packages are a godsend if only as a bargaining ploy for women. Without them, most threats would be empty. Marry someone who is not into sport and your leverage is as far as I can see very tricky indeed. Sport has its uses.

MAKING BEDS

What is astonishing about making beds is that women make such a great big meal of it, and men really do not. For women, a bed is not made unless cushions are plumped, bottom sheets are straightened, eiderdowns are pulled up and realigned, curtains are opened, tie-backs on and washing taken down into the holding area for the washing machine. No-one is expecting a Hoover or a dust, or a general spring-clean, but this is the minimum, It is only then that the bed is made.

Making the bed is not, emphatically NOT, just vaguely pulling up the duvet towards the wall. Maddeningly, it is very difficult to argue that making the bed 'woman style' – and fulfilling all the above criteria – is irrefutably the correct way, since there is no safety issue; although you could seek to find one and if you do then we want to know about it. Maddeningly, the clever spouse simply says that he doesn't mind if he comes home from a day at work to find the curtains only vaguely open and the duvet half off the bed, because in a couple of hours you are going to draw the curtains again and get back into bed.

It is not logical. Not logical is the Exocet in male argument: their weapon of mass destruction, for they can argue that bed making as we understand it is illogical, that picking up dirty washing is illogical – 'just do it once a week and take it all down together, and what is the logical point of a scatter cushion or a tie-back anyway?'

They know that when they throw down this kind of domestic gauntlet they are putting their finger on the button of household nuclear war. Result. Scatter cushions are thrown and a top-of-the-range argument ensues. Ditto with the washing-up. You can scream and scream and scream until you make yourself sick that he doesn't actually wash up anything difficult but simply leaves it to soak, or doesn't do the work surface or leaves something next to the bin without actually putting it into the bin, but it won't get you anywhere. The more you do it and wash it up and clean it up, the less likely he is to do it; same with the kids. The trouble is delegation is the only real way forward and with delegation comes one major problem for most women. No-one else does anything properly. And so nothing gets delegated at all.

Men are very good indeed at simply not doing anything, or leaving something for so long that by the time they get round to doing it the need has gone away. Which is clever. It's called laziness.

THE DAILY PROVIDING, PREPARING AND SERVING OF FOOD

Women cook on a daily basis, which is why we're sick to death of it. It's not just the cooking bit, it's the remembering to take the recycled plastic bags to the supermarket, finding a pound coin to release a trolley from the pound, having to ask the idiot boy where they've hidden the Worcester sauce, then getting to the till and realising you've left your purse at home.

Hurrah. What a perfect excuse for a takeaway. Unfortunately, one cannot live on takeaways alone, as this leads to bankruptcy and obesity – never a good mix.

The fact is for at least six nights a week, fifty-two weeks a year, women have to think, buy and prepare an evening meal; that is 312 evening meals. Add to that breakfasts and packed lunches (not to mention birthday and Christmas specials). Is it any wonder that women's lips curl at the sight of Nigella?

The thing is, families have a habit of throwing spanners into your menu plans, teenagers become vegetarians overnight, husbands get told by their doctors to lay off the dairy, you get bored stupid with mince. What's left to cook? And don't say fish: it makes the house smell.

Women are caught on the horns of the 'what are we going to eat tonight?' dilemma on a daily basis. This is why you see middle-aged females dithering in the supermarket aisles. You can almost hear their internal conversations. 'Well, Hannah won't eat sausages and we had cauliflower cheese two nights ago. I could do a tuna bake but Josh hates it; quiche is nice, but I don't like it, and we can't have pizza again.' I'm surprised more of us don't crack up in Sainsbury's. Thank God for pesto.

Men and cooking

We discussed men and cooking in a previous chapter. The thing is, even if they are quite adept in the kitchen, even if they really like cooking and list it as one of their hobbies, the truth is most middle-aged men cook once in a blue moon. They have three special dishes that they do really well, which tend to be complicated and require lots of ingredients that you don't normally have in your cupboards. If meat is involved, the meat will have to come from an organic farmers' market and the cut will be so big you will have to go out and buy an industrial roasting tray. The man will take over the kitchen and lay everything out. He will not use the same knife to chop two different vegetables.

The man will serve the meal in style, with candles and napkins. It will be utterly delicious, a fact that must be relayed with every mouthful. After the meal the man will expect you to phone some of your friends and tell them about his expertise in the kitchen (after you've stacked the dishwasher and mopped the floor of course).

For several weeks after 'the meal', the man will still be talking about how he thinks his extra clove of garlic made 'all the difference'. Your family – 'the traitors' – will remember dad's meal for months afterwards and mention it frequently, especially when shovelling down some third-rate pasta dish you've plonked on the table.

'Oh, remember when dad made that meal. Wasn't it fantastic? He's such an amazing cook.'

This will make you want to lie on the floor biting tea towels.

ERRANDS

Errands aren't as fashionable as they once were but now and then you still need someone to go and borrow an egg from next door or pop a letter in the post. Men can be a bit forgetful. You can send him next door to fetch an egg and he will come back three hours later having watched a DVD of the first series of *Life on Mars*. Equally, if you ask him to post a letter, make sure there is nothing to distract him between your house and the letter box. I once asked my partner to post a letter and on the way to the post box he saw a secondhand Saab up for sale at a very reasonable price. 'What about my letter?' I asked. 'What letter?' he replied.

Of course, when you want them to be forgetful, they suddenly turn into Mr Memory.

LITTLE JOBS

Quite often there will be little jobs that need to be done around the house that neither of you will be capable of doing. In an ideal world a man should not be able to marry a woman until he has passed some kind of 'little jobs about the house' course. This course would cover basic DIY skills, handling a drill, wiring a plug, etc. For example, the final exam might involve removing a door from its hinges with an electric screwdriver/ finding the trip switch in the cupboard under the stairs/tuning in a new telly and rigging up an iPod. Any man who had not completed this course would not be allowed into a hardware shop, never mind matrimony.

Sometimes as couples we have to know when to call in the experts. This is galling when you have to pay a £50 call-out fee for someone to come and put a new washer on a tap.

Of course, it's not just the man of the house who is supposed to be able to handle 'little jobs about the house'. Women are often called upon to do things that are supposed to come naturally – but for some of us don't. Little jobs that women are meant to be able to do that actually make them hop and swear:

Remove splinters without gouging great holes in the skin
Sew on a button without leaving bloodstains
Run up some curtains (Ha!)
Remove ink/egg/hair dye/nail varnish/chewing gum from
    carpet
Clean up pet accidents
Stay in for man who is coming to fix the dishwasher – some
    time, could be any time – between now and next Wednesday
Find things. Of all the little jobs a woman is expected to do, this
    is the most time-consuming. No-one in your house can find
    anything. This is because they do not look; it is your job to
    do the looking. Things you will find yourself looking for will
    include 'that letter from the bank', an important phone

number, swimming stuff, goggles, pink tights, that purple
eye-liner, a book about the Reformation, your sanity

SHOPPING

What is it with men? They don't notice what is already in the fridge.
Women see that there are sausages that should have been used up
yesterday and they make sausage and mash, but men ignore that
and buy some fillet steaks. Men are equally incapable of buying
washing-up liquid, dishwasher salt, loo rolls or bread.

In a way it was so much easier when women didn't go out to
work and just did nest building and keeping house and childcare.
That way the lines of responsibility were very carefully drawn, but
now they are desperately blurred; not even looking after the car is
his responsibility.

OK, may we just say now that it is wrong on every level to see
a woman washing a car. It is fine for a woman to drive through a car
wash, it's even better that she pays some lad to wash it by hand
whilst she is in the supermarket, but it is a very depressing sight to
see a woman struggling with a hose, bucket and chamois leather in
her own drive. Washing the car is possibly the most horrible household chore and even if he bought me a Mercedes convertible I still
wouldn't do it – not even if it was covered in bird poo.

PERSONAL ADMIN

Clearly whoever does the DIY is exempt from personal admin.
Personally I would prefer to unblock the sceptic tank than do
personal admin, which is the only real tangible example of why
two different houses is a disadvantage – for everything else it works.

Basically the rule of thumb with personal admin is that the
most organised person should take charge. This is best decided
by star sign: hence one of the best reasons for marrying a Virgo.

SLEEPING

The trouble with sleeping with someone else is that you have someone else's sleep to compare with, which is OK if you're the one that sleeps well, but if you sleep badly – and let's face it as we get older this happens – and you sleep next to someone who sleeps like a baby, this can be irritating. And if they have kept you awake all night because they snore like a hedge trimmer then this is very irritating indeed.

One of the things about being a long-term Grumpy Old Couple is that there is never any dithering about who should sleep on which side. Your 'sides' have been long ordained.

On the Grumpy Old Woman's side (in my case the left – J.E.), on top of the bedside table will be a pile of books (healthy mix of Richard and Judy Book Club and Orange Prize nominees), various anti-ageing creams, glasses, smelly candle and photo of 'happy family'. On his bedside table the Grumpy Old Man will hoard a few books about war, his reading glasses, the remote control (which he arm wrestles you for every night) and a packet of biscuits in case his blood sugar levels fall dramatically during the night.

Snoring

This is something both of you are going to have to put up with. All you can hope for is your increasing deafness reaps its own reward.

MONEY

More couples argue about money than anything else – that's because men want to buy stupid things like golf clubs and beer, and women need shoes.

Personally I think there should be two entirely different currencies – boy currency for boring things and lady lolly for treats. OK, maybe I haven't thought this one through. All I know about women and money is that we are capable of extreme levels of parsimony (for example, eating nothing but baked potatoes for weeks on end) followed by extreme levels of extravagance when we will do something like buy a pair of sandals for 350 quid, which we can't walk properly in.

Men and money

Men are even weirder about money than women. They can't see the problem with wanting to spend £70,000 on a silly car, whereas women know that if they have a £70,000 car they will scratch it to pieces every time they turn a corner in a multi-storey car park. Men on the other hand don't envisage having to ever take it into a multi-storey car park. They can only imagine themselves driving it with the top down and loads of girls on the back seat with no seat belts on.

This is one of the biggest differences between men and women. When men fantasise, they fantasise recklessly. Women fantasise, but even if Daniel Craig came to pick us up in a Lamborghini we'd still put our seat belt on and say, 'Actually, Dan love, it's a bit nippy and I've just had me hair done. Can you pop the roof back on? Ooh, yes, and be careful as you go round the corner – it's a nasty bend.'

RULES FOR A HARMONIOUS GRUMPY HOUSEHOLD

These can be cut out and laminated. Remember, these are just some guidelines; you're welcome to make up lots of rules of your own.

House rules

Muddy shoes removed before walking across new taupe carpet.
They should be placed on newspaper in the vestibule and

dealt with once the mud has dried with a stiff wire brush

The new cream sofa should be treated as if it has been marked off from the rest of the sitting room with incident tape. It's a no-go area: do not think of sitting, eating or drinking on it. However, when guests arrive usher them to the new sofa and try not to wince when they ask for red wine

Toe-nail clippings to be deposited and flushed in the lavatory, not lined up neatly on the window ledge – or kept weirdly in a matchbox

Bedside lights should either have synchronised switch-off times or be angled to cause the non-reader the least inconvenience possible. If, after ten minutes, the non-reader is still being disturbed by the reader's light it is permissible to have a discussion as to whether the book is worth reading late into the night. Award-winning books are valid, magazines are not.

Garden rules

Men, you can't make her do weeding; there is such a condition as 'being allergic to doing boring things in the garden'

Men, if you make her do horrible gardening jobs, then you must pay for a weekly manicure

If you've got a pond and the pump/filter thing keeps breaking do not spend more than £300 having it fixed. Once this sum has been reached forget about the stupid pond. Fill it with sand and at least it will be more useful now as the foxes will have somewhere nice to crap

If you are going to throw slugs/snails into the next-door garden, be prepared for them to throw them back

Garage rules

Respect each other's tools: ladies do not use his drill for defrosting the fridge, men do not use her tweezers for picking shards of a very small broken bulb out of the glove compartment of your car

However bad things get, do not commit suicide in the garage; it's very upsetting for the other half. Do it off the premises, either in a wood a long way away or by jumping off a tower block in another town. A bit of consideration, that's all we want

Ditto: women should not kill themselves by putting their head Sylvia Plath style into the oven. Every time he heats up a shepherd's pie, he's going to have flashbacks. There's no need to be selfish

Shed rules

If it's his shed, women keep out

If it's her shed, men keep out

Car rules

If it's her car never ever retune the radio. It took her seven hours to find Radio 4. Just leave it, whatever you do – and do not retune to Radio 5 Live

Do not put the seat back. She doesn't know where the button for getting it to come forward is. OK, so you think she drives like a monkey up a stick, she thinks you drive like a lunatic

NB: It is pointless to attempt to see whether your bottom looks big in a rear-view mirror. It is physically impossible – trust me, I have tried.

Buying a Sat Nav could save your relationship. In the old days, men would rather run out of petrol than ask for directions, now you've got a third party to blame if you end up facing the wrong way down the M11.

Fact

Women can't read maps. We can't even fold them up properly without getting into a right old tizz.

Most men can't read maps but they still think they know better.

Fridge rules

Do not put an empty milk/juice carton back in the fridge

Do not ignore the cracked egg when you are thinking of making an omelette

Tins do not need to go in the fridge until they have been opened and half their contents used; it is best to decant this leftover product into a dish and put clingfilm over it

Do not get attached to this leftover product; throw it away after two days

Do not wipe out the fridge with a smelly cloth

Check the salad tray for signs of green slime

Don't pretend that onion hasn't gone off; just put a rubber glove on, pick it up and throw it away

Mayonnaise tastes better when it's cold

Ditto white wine – make sure there is some in there

RETIREMENT

'In sickness and in health'

The trouble with having the old man off work and under your feet for more than a couple of days is that it feels like some weird rehearsal for the future, that time of unspoken dread when there is no place to go to in the morning and there's a brand-new carriage clock tick-tocking on the mantelpiece. Yes, what everyone has got to remember is that the second you pass forty-five you are closer to sixty than to thirty and we all know what sixty means. (Well, that's what it used to mean. Let's face it, most of us these days are going to have to work till we drop, but let's not get bogged down with semantics.)

Retirement – a new beginning or the beginning of the end?

The trouble with no-one having a job for life any more is that retirement can strike at any time. Ideally you want your man in gainful employment until at least sixty-five when he should then find some part-time jobette that will keep him in pocket money and most importantly from under your feet.

Preparations should be made for retirement – sheds and ponds are good distractions. A pond is a bit like having another child: wet, smelly and more trouble than it's worth. It is a good project for a man to take on, as he must first dig it, then line it, then fill it with water. At this point he will feel a sense of achievement, which is great apart from the fact that he will at this point turn into a pond bore.

The worst-case scenario will involve your retired man buying *Pond Life* and catalogues featuring water features. A water feature is a nice idea, even if the retired man has prostate problems. However, they are notoriously tricky to install and the mental hospitals of Great Britain are chocca with men of a certain age suffering from pond-related psychosis – so much so that medical experts simply refer to the condition by the initials PRP.

Of course not everyone succumbs to PRP. There are a few lucky men who will have positive pond experiences to the point where they feel confident enough to buy koi carp. Just a word of warning here: koi carp are expensive; not as expensive as race horses but a carp is never going to win the 3.10 at Haymarket. See what I'm saying? Basically you don't want to find yourself being a carp widow.

Remember: the cost of a mature carp is in the region of 400 quid! It's no good buying just one. It will just go mad and die of loneliness. And the things you will need include:

Filtration system
Anti-heron edge to pond

Koi protein meal mix, containing worms, crustaceans, brewer's
    yeast, garlic and honey
Aquatic disinfectant tablets designed to prevent outbreaks of
    bacterial infections
Sock net

The way I see it, what's wrong with a bit of old-fashioned frogspawn
and a fountain in the shape of a small boy weeing?

The shed
Again the shed can be a dangerous source of one-upmanship
between men of a certain age.

Sheds come in all shapes and sizes but traditionally they are
wooden and should smell of linseed oil and rotting apples. It is
common practice to stash porn in the shed. This is fine but nothing
hard core; in fact eighties' copies of *Razzle* are preferable. Other
items a good shed should contain include some tools, a work bench,
plant pots, balls of string, some pots of paint, a radio, a comfy

deckchair with cushion and either a ginger-beer plant or some home brew.

A shed should only be tidied by a male hand. It should not feature curtains or a bed – if it does, he's basically moved out.

Shed v conservatory

Just as every man wants a shed, many women feel the need for a conservatory. What they want is somewhere vaguely tropical to nod off in every afternoon whilst listening to a nice play on Radio 4. In reality, the conservatory will become a source of misery for many women as the glass will never be clean enough and however much newspaper and vinegar you use there will always be a nasty smear in a certain light. That's another thing, the light will be too bright – necessitating the purchase of complicated blinds, which will be so expensive that you will have to forgo your annual foreign holiday to pay for them. Spending two weeks sitting in your stuffy conservatory in August, blinds or no blinds, is no substitute for Fuengirola and you will end up resenting your conservatory – especially if it's one of those that gets so hot your *Take a Break* magazine turns to pulp in your hand.

ANNIVERSARIES – AND GIFTS IN GENERAL

The thing with anniversaries is that they are not really that important unless one or other of the parties involved forgets or is carelessly inattentive, or even over-attentive and then they become very important indeed. Some people celebrate romantically the day they met but most of us have to be more concise and celebrate our wedding or civil partnership which is neater and better recorded for evidence.

The trouble with anniversaries is that they bring with them the need for presents, and presents between partners – as we know – are very tricky indeed. However, here are some easy-to-follow rules:

Women want jewellery or (expensive) flowers. They don't want chocolate (makes them fat) or sexy underwear (makes them feel fat), and they want the receipt. Anything 'useful' for the house or kitchen is not only undesired but is grounds for divorce as recognised by the courts of law. Gifts of food processors, Hoovers or saucepans all constitute 'unreasonable behaviour', which will take you right up to the top of the queue divorce-wise.

Men want something unique and romantic. They want to receive something which indicates that their 'snuffle bum' has put in some time and research. They would be offended if they were offered the receipt. They don't want novelty socks, a practical shirt or a car accessory. Men want days out messing around in racing cars. Their best present in the world would be to be taken round the *Top Gear* racing track with The Stig. They dream of Jeremy Clarkson telling them they beat Simon Cowell.

Paper, zinc, glass, etc. anniversaries

1 **PAPER** GOOD nice stationery from Smythson, the posh shop where David Cameron's Mrs works. BAD doilies

2 **COTTON** GOOD six exquisite napkins from Liberty. BAD pants from the market

3 **LEATHER** GOOD a gorgeous handbag from Mulberry. BAD a leather-look bag from Primark

4 **LINEN** GOOD Egyptian-cotton pillow cases. BAD a linen basket

5 **WOOD** GOOD a lovely carved bowl. BAD a stick

6 **IRON** GOOD a really lovely set of Le Creuset. BAD a 9-iron (don't blame us if she hits you over the head with it)

7 **WOOL** GOOD cashmere sweater. BAD a bobble hat

8 **BRONZE** GOOD a sequin top in a bronze colour. BAD some fake tan

9 **POTTERY** GOOD Wedgwood. BAD something you made yourself

10 **TIN** GOOD a new car. BAD a tin of baked beans

11 **STEEL** GOOD brand-new stainless-steel Smeg fridge with ice-making compartment. BAD stainless steel ice bucket or pickle fork

12 **SILK** GOOD a kimono-style housecoat.
BAD crotchless panties

13 **LACE** GOOD posh underwear. BAD curtains

14 **IVORY** Um: this is actually illegal now

15 **CRYSTAL** GOOD glassware. BAD some rubbish healing rock

20 **CHINA** GOOD two tickets to ... BAD a takeaway

25 **SILVER** GOOD a pen. BAD a sixpence

30 **PEARL** GOOD necklace and matching earrings.
BAD expecting pearl necklace back

35 **CORAL** GOOD necklace again. BAD a bag of scallops from fishmonger

40 **RUBY** GOOD a ring. BAD a curry

45 **SAPPHIRE** GOOD more proper jewellery. BAD bottle of Sapphire gin

50 **GOLD** GOOD more jewellery. BAD a box of Ferrero Rocher

55 **EMERALD** GOOD more jewellery. BAD some cheap green-coloured glass thing pretending to be an emerald

60 **DIAMOND** GOOD more sparkly jewellery. BAD can of Diamond White Cider (only ever drunk on park benches)

70 **PLATINUM** GOOD more jewellery. BAD a duck-billed platypus – he got it wrong

80th **OAK** GOOD a bench for the two of you to sit on in the garden. BAD an acorn

SOME MORE GOLDEN RULES
OF STAYING TOGETHER

Be nice to one another now and again. Satisfy yourself that they are not perfect but at least you know where they've been.

Small gestures work just as well as big ones. A cup of peppermint tea and some Nurofen when she's 'not right' will have you back in her good books for a week. Tell her she 'looks nice' and that you like that 'tunic' – even if 'tunic' is the wrong word.

Men need affection. Remember he needs patting and stroking and reminding 'he's a good boy'. If you don't do this his eyes will become dull and his coat won't shine. Don't shoot him down in flames even if it's a 'daft idea'. At least let him tell you what the idea is before you pull 'that face'. Don't make him a horrible packed lunch – that's one of the lowest things a woman can do.

Remember

Look before you leap. OK, you might be fed up to the back teeth with him, but before you leave, have a quick look at what else is on offer ... you might change your mind.

7 · Despair

DIVORCE

We've all thought about it, especially when he uses the corner of a credit card to pick wax out of his ear, but seriously can you be bothered?

Obviously if you're really unhappy and you can't either rely on him dying any time soon or think of a way of killing him without having to go to prison, then get it over and done with, but for most of us it's usually better the devil you know.

Can you think of anything worse than going through all that dating malarkey again? OK, so he's got a miniature train set in the attic and wears a cardigan, and OK she uses your razor for her underarms and never wears those suspenders you bought her – but it could be worse. At least he's not taking ketamine and sleeping with prostitutes – not that train sets and cardies and ketamine and call girls are mutually exclusive. Takes all sorts ... and at least she's not on the vodka and tonic in front of GMTV – well, not most days anyway.

As we all know, the only people who always benefit from divorce are the lawyers. By the way, if you've accidentally married one of them, then divorce is probably quite a good idea.

Grounds for divorce for her

Forgetting your birthday – unless he's had a recent nasty blow to the head

Sleeping with the cleaning woman – especially when you're the one who pays her

Sleeping with your best friend; he could at least have had the decency to have gone for the silly slag at number 43

Doing jigsaw puzzle on the dining-room table and sulking when you ask him to move it

Liking the dog more than you and not trying to hide the fact

Only having one joke and telling it badly

Wearing really horrible shorts

Any combination of the above

Grounds for divorce for him

Not shaving her legs even when she is wearing shorts or on the beach where your best friend will see her

Giving you a CD for your birthday which really she wanted, and then putting it on her iPod before you even get a chance to play it

Forgetting that you don't like liver, again

Ruining your one good joke

Wearing shorts at all

Any combination of the above

Clearly if divorce is really and truly inevitable, then couples should be made to sort it out between themselves or have their heads knocked together. One of you gets to sort the assets into two piles and the other chooses which half to take – there – easy – who needs solicitors. Then we can all be civil about it and have a nice divorce party, which is clearly the way forward. There's a whole new market for someone out there: divorce cakes, divorce balloons, divorce presents … it's wide open.

REASONS WHY A RELATIONSHIP GOES WRONG FOR THE GRUMPY MIDDLE-AGED WOMAN

Gifts

He buys you kitchen equipment for your birthday, This is fine if
it's one of those expensive Gaggia coffee machines but not if
it's a selection of balloon whisks

When we say we want something for the bath we don't mean a
nice big bottle of Cif limescale remover. We mean smellies
that come in nice packaging; i.e. not from the supermarket
and not when it's two for the price of one. And if it has the
word 'value' on it, frankly it's grounds for changing the locks

My dad once bought my mum a KitKat and ate half of it while she
went downstairs to make a cup of tea – wrong on all levels

Any lotion or potion that guarantees to get rid of fine lines or
liver spots; you're not supposed to notice, you fool

Anything that is red and made of nylon – she's not a whore

Anything technical that needs wiring-in or programming; we
      don't want Sat Navs, iPods or BlackBerries; in fact we'd
      rather have another bloody scented candle
Never ever buy anything from the garage

God, here is an idiot-proof cut-out-and-keep guide to buying gifts
for the Mrs:

Cashmere – go for a black V-neck from Marks
Jo Malone anything and don't give me, 'but I live in Ormskirk';
      you can buy online
A year's subscription to a glossy magazine
Coloured leather gloves
Nice stationery
'Your song' on vinyl
A Nigel Slater cookery book
A great big diamond – oh go on

REASONS WHY IT ALL GOES WRONG FOR MEN

She doesn't want sex, she doesn't like golf and she won't let him
buy a shed. She is therefore a miserable cow and mad to boot.

Fair enough. Try and find a woman who is really into sex, golf
and sheds and I will show you lesbian.

THINK BEFORE YOU LEAP

The sad thing about a lot of marriages that get into trouble is that
a lot of the upset is avoidable. Just practise saying 'sorry' in the
mirror, go on ... as if you really mean it. Practise until you have a face
and a voice that really look and sound convincing. Now go and
apologise, but just make sure he can't see that you've got your
fingers crossed behind your back.

Some couples get stuck in a rut and mistake boredom for unhappiness. Before you split up, make sure boredom isn't at the root of your problem. Do something mad together, get on the wrong bus, eat somewhere you've never tried before, go for a walk and make yourselves hold hands. If the thought of holding his hand makes you feel sick and vice versa then it's probably all over.

Imagine being married to your best friend's other half. If that makes you feel grateful for what you've got, then there is happiness at the end of the tunnel. However, if it makes you feel all gooey inside and a bit hot and flustered then everyone's in trouble.

Statistically two in five marriages end up in divorce, which still means three out of five don't. Lots of marriages go through 'a bad patch' with symptoms ranging from one of you sleeping on the sofa through to one of you sleeping on the sofa at a mate's house.

Other 'bad patch' signs:

Sulky silences at the breakfast table broken only by banging down of teapot and heavy sighs

Not getting round to washing his favourite shirt – and deliberately leaving it stinking at the bottom of the laundry basket

Not making his favourite meal for three months even though you're secretly craving it

'Forgetting' to put that tile back on in the bathroom even though the tub of grout is 'just sitting there'

Not reminding her that her favourite programme is on (very very very spiteful) and then, as soon as it's over, saying, 'Isn't that thing you like on tonight?'

Hiding her book/mascara/lipsalve/handbag – this is very cruel as all middle-aged women think they might have Alzheimer's, and playing games like this could push her over the edge

WHEN IS A BAD PATCH TERMINAL?

I think it's quite an interesting sign when you suddenly don't feel the need to have that person at the epicentre of your life.
KATHRYN FLETT

There's always a moment in relationships when I know it's over and that's when I'm aware of him chewing at breakfast time … whereas before I wouldn't have even noticed and suddenly I'm going 'I can't stand that noise.' That means it's over.
GERMAINE GREER

Some marriages are like ancient dogs with cataracts and tumours: it is kinder to put them out of their misery.

OK, so you can't have your wife or husband put to sleep, there isn't a vet in the land who will agree to that (however many fivers you wave under their nose). But you don't need to prolong the agony. Get out while both of you still have time to find happiness elsewhere (despite this being the last thing either of you wants for the other).

DIVORCE AND CHILDREN

It doesn't matter how old your children are, they will still be upset if the two of you decide to separate. I know a 36-year-old man who, when his parents split up, started wetting the bed. This in turn led to the breakdown of his own marriage. What a sorry state of affairs all round.

Try not to break up when your children are doing exams. They will only use the break up as an excuse not to do any revision and fail the whole blinking lot.

Do not break the news on anyone's birthday, including the hampster's and, however hard it might be, don't let the cat out of the bag on Xmas Day.

Remember the mathematical equation of divorce is that everything is divided by two = half of what you had before. Think this through before you start looking up 'solicitors' in the Yellow Pages.

THE SPORT OF REMARRIAGE

Competing with his ex

Remember: competition between wives and ex-wives is what keeps milliners going at family weddings – the bigger the hat, the bigger the rivalry.

For some reason, when men marry wife No. 2 they tend to go for the complete opposite of what they had before. This is why so many second wives tend to be young, blonde bundles of fun. What many men don't take into consideration is that going for something 'completely different' is a bit like choosing something exotic in a restaurant. It might look fantastic, it might even taste really nice, but when you're in the grip of advanced indigestion some hours later you will wish you'd gone for your usual steak and chips.

Competing with her ex

Just make sure you've got a better car. If you can't afford a better car, play the Green card.

Imaginary boyfriends

Of course the worst scenario in the world is when he's managed to 'move on': in other words gets himself a new floosie and you – the wronged wife – have not.

Beware the danger of reverting back to your 15-year-old self and inventing an imaginary boyfriend.

When you are young and not so grumpy, you think that men are the be-all and end-all. All you want is a boyfriend and you practise kissing your posters and making love to your pillow. You're frankly not all that fussy, let's face it. As long as he's not made of paper or polyester then it's got to be better than nothing.

Of course we were wrong. Any bloke is not better than no bloke. To be honest you're better off with a nice imaginary boyfriend than some of the idiots out there.

The pros to having an imaginary boyfriend:

He doesn't come round and use up all your lavatory paper. What is it with men and loo paper? Why are they so extravagant; after all it doesn't grow on trees ... er, well, yes it does but that's beside the point.

The fact he doesn't exist makes it less likely that he's going to go off with your younger sister/best friend/brother.

He won't argue about what to watch on the television; the remote control is yours, all yours.

He won't expect a cooked meal every night. In fact, because he doesn't need to eat, neither do you, so you may even lose some weight. Hoorah. See, I told you it was a good idea.

Buying him expensive birthday and Xmas gifts is pointless. Great, you can spend the money on shoes instead.

He's not going to complain if you come to bed with hairy legs and neither will he keep you awake grinding his teeth or farting like a one-man farting machine.

He's not going to let you down at the works Xmas do. Obviously he's not going to turn up either but that's only because his imaginary appendix has exploded.

Your mum won't hate his guts. How can she? She's never met him and she's not going to.

His mother won't think he's too good for you, how can he be?

Because he's imaginary you can pretend he used to go out with Jennifer Aniston but chucked her for you.

See, there's no harm in it, as long as you don't start talking to him on the bus.

OTHER STRANGE RELATIONSHIPS MIDDLE-AGED WOMEN CAN'T BE TRUSTED NOT TO TRY

The death-row prisoner

So just because you know where he is all the time is no reason to get involved. OK, there are pros: he's not going to get under your feet and steal your lavatory paper. Cons: he's a con.

The Masai warrior

Oh God, have you never read *Take a Break*? This will so end in tears. He's twenty years younger than you, so – how can we put this nicely – he's after your money you silly cow. OK, so there's the odd exception that doesn't end up with all your friends shaking their heads and saying, 'I told you so,' but you wait, if it does last, then he'll want his family to visit – all thirty-six of them plus goats.

The reformed bad boy

This is the type of fellow that combs his hair in public: to be avoided at all cost. Can you really relax in the arms of a man who has the name Brenda tattooed on one bicep and Stacey on the other, especially if your name is Annabelle and you come from the Home Counties? How can we put this nicely – he's after your money you silly cow!

Mummy's little soldier

Fifty-six and not wed, still lives with his mother … You think you can change him, you think you're strong enough? So does he, that's why he's after you. He wants a nice, strong, sensible woman who can lift mother in and out of the bath while he drinks hot chocolate and watches *Dr Who* videos in his pyjamas.

RIDICULOUS RELATIONSHIPS GRUMPY OLD MEN CAN'T BE TRUSTED NOT TO EMBARK UPON

Tart with a heart

One of those women who looks best in electric light, slightly scary in daylight, but has a marvellous cleavage. The problem with the tart with a heart is that she never had the sense to use contraception and will have nine kids by different dads, some of whom will have been in prison, all of whom will want to beat you up. The trouble is she's a fantasy and not practical partner material. Yes, she might be very willing in the bedroom but she won't think to change the Hoover bag. The tart with the heart will have some rather disturbing habits; for example, she will put her cigarettes out in Fray Bentos meat-pie dishes, Fray Bentos being the only thing she can cook. Your relationship will end in tears and rickets.

The much younger woman

Every middle-aged man, particularly if his marriage has broken down, needs to go out with a much younger woman at least once. Once should be enough to realise how stultifyingly dull they are, unless of course you've managed to pick up one who is studying Medieval French at Cambridge, though let's face it, unless you look like George Clooney (which even George Clooney doesn't most days), that isn't very likely. Very young women really only fancy quite well-off blokes. Basically, if you haven't got a yacht they will be disappointed; if you really think she's interested in you for your personality give her the choice between dinner out of a bucket, courtesy of KFC, or a night at Nobu. This relationship will leave you looking foolish, particularly if you make the mistake of taking her clubbing and dancing in public. That noise you can hear? It's people laughing.

The foreign beauty

She won't look like anything you've ever got into bed with before. She won't have straggly pubes or bitten toe-nails, she will have a vast selection of exotic nightwear in chocolate satin and cream lace, and she will look posher than a Wall's Magnum – but when you tell her this she will not be amused. That will be the problem: she won't laugh at anything you say or do. She will want to take everything seriously including making love. She will expect you to know all the tricks and never get your arm trapped under her bum. When you do that thing when you honk her nipples as if they were old-fashioned hooters and you make that stupid parping sound, she will give you a look that will ensure you don't get another erection for a very long time indeed. The only antidote to this kind of relationship is to go out with someone really stupid who thinks that you are a genius because you know how to put petrol in a car.

The very silly woman

The very silly woman is usually kind and good at cuddling. However, she will talk in a baby voice and collect china pigs or frogs. She will also have a menagerie of stuffed animals on the bed but, despite this, she will be vegetarian and very squeamish about food. If she had her way she'd just eat Dairylea triangles and choccie bickies. The very silly woman will never have read a novel in her life. However, she will refer to the Sunday supplement magazines as 'books'. She will be a sucker for romantic comedies and will genuinely believe that Jennifer Lopez is a really good actress. She will also get confused between actors and their on-screen personas, and though she is religiously fanatical about the soaps her favourite programme is *Loose Women* because the celebrities are all so funny and clever. The very silly woman can't drive, swim or ride a bike; mind you, you can have hours of fun watching her try to catch a ball.

BE PRACTICAL

Instead of entering some strange or ridiculous relationship, a better bet would be someone who is going to be more on your grumpy wavelength. We might as well be practical here, Grumpy Old Women need Grumpy Old Men and it's no good pretending otherwise.

Characteristics of the Grumpy Old Man

He will like Formula One/golf/rugby/certain football matches and beer (however, he is not a hooligan)

He will stir his sugar into his tea and then put the wet teaspoon directly back into the sugar bowl – which is a bit hooliganny

He might make a grunting noise when he bends down to tie his shoelaces

He will not look good in skinny jeans; however, he will look good in a corduroy jacket

He won't change the bed very often, not even in the guest bedroom – and doesn't think anyone will notice

He won't know what to put in a shopping basket in the super-market; you will see him dither as he's not quite sure which are the Jerusalem artichokes and which are globe – ah, he's quite sweet really

How to spot a potential Grumpy Old Woman mate

Her car might be broken, but it's more likely to have run out of petrol

She will not know how to put your number into her mobile phone, so she will write it down on the back of an envelope in eyebrow pencil

She will only have used the eyebrow pencil on one eyebrow

She might be buying something a bit nostalgic from a car-boot sale, like an old *Jackie* annual – ah, she's quite sweet really

WATCH THE BAGGAGE

The thing about coupling up in later life (sorry, that makes it sound like you are trying to attach a caravan to an old estate car, which in some respects you are) is that both of you will have baggage.

Even if you haven't been married or had children, you will still have a past. Your grumpy new love will be obsessed by this past and will probably snoop for photos of ex-lovers every time you turn your back. She will be particularly sarky about that snap of you with your arm around the Norwegian girl in the yellow bikini on the beach in Rhodes back in '86.

Some people have more baggage than others and sometimes the baggage comes in the form of flesh and blood children.

Women and their children

Women love their children: this is the only thing that makes it possible to change nappies. Unfortunately loving other people's children is not always easy, especially when they are sly-eyed feral teenage monsters. Pros: at least they're out of the nappy stage. Cons: they will still be puking, thanks to alcopop abuse.

Teenage boy monsters will try and tap you for money and say things like, 'Yeah, well, you're not my dad.'

Teenage girl monsters will look at you as if you're some kind of freak, tap you for money and say stuff like, 'Yeah, well, you're not my dad and anyway you're really sad.' Their mum will pretend they're just teasing, they aren't.

The only way you can get them to like you is to buy them stuff, or go and pick them up from the police station and never ever tell their mum. Eventually a combination of buying them stuff and blackmail will succeed in winning them round.

Warning

You really have to love someone to take on their kids.

BEING SINGLE AND OVER 40

*I think that it's really important that, as long as you are breathing,
you stay open to the possibilities.*   JENNI TRENT HUGHES

I think we get more than one shot at it.   KATHRYN FLETT

Lots of people end up having to start again in their forties, fifties,
sixties, seventies, eighties or even nineties. No marriage comes
with a lifetime guarantee, not even a non-stick pan can promise
that. The thought of having to get dressed up and go clubbing in
some absurd shoes, or having to join the local tennis club to try to
meet people is for the grumpy a chasteningly scary prospect.
However bad your spouse is, he or she will seem like a dream when
you are faced with being back on the dating scene. For one thing you
will know where he or she has been, whereas people in their forties
and fifties in nightclubs could be very odd people indeed. Face it: the
ones with the straightforward and squeaky-clean pasts – like widows
or widowers – are snapped up within minutes of the funeral.

The sad fact is that sometimes relationships go wrong, people
get divorced, wives lose their husbands either in B&Q or to some
nasty disease, or worse ... to another woman – and we have to look
around for someone new. This is not as easy as you might hope.
Seeing people you fancy is easy, finding out where they live and
accidentally bumping into them without being a scary stalker is
the tricky bit.

Lots of people use online dating services or, if you're a bit more
traditional, the lonely hearts columns in the newspapers. It might
seem a bit like playing pimps and prostitutes but if the *Guardian*
does it, it's got to be OK.

It would be nice to be able to meet new partners through friends
but the fact is there just aren't enough single people – by which
we mean men to go round. Where are they all? Going out with
younger women – that's where.

PLACES TO MEET NEW PEOPLE
Online dating
This can be like a very sophisticated version of having a pen pal. You have no idea what he/she looks like and sometimes it's better left that way.

Friends Reunited
Might as well be known as DivorcesRUs.com. This is one of the dangers of having too much time on your hands and a computer. I tell you, you'd be better off getting addicted to online gambling. The consequences will be more or less the same: you will lose your house and your family and there is no guarantee that you will be any happier or better off than you were when you first started meddling.

The trouble with Friends Reunited is that you emotionally regress to whatever age you were when you first fancied X, which is usually fifteen, and there are reasons why 15-year-olds aren't allowed to get married in this country. Ideally, you should both just get it out of your system, share a bottle of cider behind a bike shed, give each other a love-bite or, if you still can't do that properly, have a snog, shake hands and move on. If possible, get your parents involved in the recreation; get them to lock you out when you come home covered in love-bites twenty minutes past your curfew. A night in the shed should soon knock some sense into you. For God's sake you're fifty.

Sports club
Pros: there is usually a bar. Cons: he/she will like sport – yawn.

If you are going to play any sport, however, go for badminton. It's a bit of a laugh and you get to say cock at the end of shuttle-cock.

Dog walking

This is good because your dogs will sniff each other's bottoms as if it were the most natural and normal thing in the world. Therefore you may too.

In the supermarket

Apparently this is all the rage. Rather like the gay scene where keys and hankies hanging from different pockets indicate different sexual preferences, there's a kind of code thing going on ... Imagine in your local Asda, for example, a pack of butter in your basket means you like it *Godfather*-style, whereas a tub of vanilla ice cream means safe traditional sex only, whilst a big can of baked beans and a squirty aerosol of cream equals very messy indeed.

Personally, I'd be looking for the bloke with a nice bottle of wine, two juicy steaks, a bag of salad and a packet of condoms – why does everything have to get so complicated?

In the car park

No, really, this is a very bad idea. You will only get your photo printed in the local paper and everyone who knows you will die of shame.

Accidentally smashing into his car

By law he is forced to ask you for your phone number. Yes, you win. This time next year you could be married again.

Let's just say, for the sake of argument, you do happen to meet someone, you will need to take them on a date. You can pay for this date by collecting money from all those so-called friends who betted you a tenner you'd never meet anyone ever again. See, already it's worthwhile.

DATES: PLACES TO GO

Places of historical interest

The great thing about the National Trust is the word 'Trust'. If I were a complete womanising bastard I would join the National Trust simply because having the sticker in my car window would lure more women into my clutches.

Middle-aged women love a good snoop around a historically interesting house. All we really want is for the bossy cow with the name badge who won't let you touch anything to bog off so we can spend a couple of hours having a really good rummage. One of my fantasies is hopping over the red rope that divides where the commoners and I go and 'the private quarters'. Obviously in my fantasy I am so popular over on the other side that the posh Lord and Lady decide to adopt me. I have had this fantasy since I was eleven.

Houses of historical interest don't have to be that historically interesting but they must have refreshments available and a gift shop to boot. No day out is ever complete without the purchase of a tea towel, a set of attractive coasters or perhaps an interesting jar of chutney. Yes, we do find chutney interesting and you blokes better sit up and take note. An interesting jar of chutney will only cost about three quid. Go on, treat her; your rewards will far outweigh the expense.

Of course it's important for the bloke not to show too much interest in the soft furnishings and William Morris wallpaper inside the house as that would be a bit gay. However, it's OK to enthuse about the landscaping of the grounds (mumble something about Capability Brown) but don't spend too much time in the lawn-mower museum in the garages round the back. She will pretend to be interested but actually she will be bored.

The wrong kind of place of historical interest

Women do not appreciate those knocked-down old castles that haven't got any walls or ceilings left. These types of things – ruins in other words – are usually on top of a windswept hill and it's impossible to know if you're in the pantry or the hall – very dull. Also, these ruin places don't tend to have tea shoppes, which either means a picnic in the car or starvation.

Picnic in the car – pros and cons

Personally, I think picnics come long after farting in a relation-ship, possibly about ten years down the line. Summer picnics with a rug in a nice park with strawberries and champagne are fine – even if you've only just met – but once the hard-boiled egg is added into the equation then the picnic is a very different proposition. There is something terribly mean about a packed lunch. If I ever worked in an office I don't think I could contemplate sexual relations with a man who brought in a packed lunch. Fair enough if he's married and has lots of children in private education – but a single, solvent, packed-lunch eater is a bit penny-pinching and therefore not attractive.

However, there are exceptions to this rule. If the packed lunch is out of the ordinary – perhaps involving rice noodles, peanuts and chicken, or tamarind – then obviously we can give him the benefit of the doubt. All I'm trying to say is: beware the man who only eats jam sandwiches.

Train museums
Bad.

IKEA
Very bad.

A walk in the park
Good, if the park has a bandstand, maybe a boating lake, a petting zoo, a gastro café (possibly licensed) or a Barbara Hepworth sculpture (note: it's always good to have some nugget of information up your sleeve when you're out and about – for example, knowing your Hepworths from your Henry Moores, but usually it's a simple case of reading the brass plaque at the bottom of the statue). Dulwich Park with an art gallery five minutes away and the village with its PizzaExpress and candle shops – ideal. This is the kind of date that could end up looking in estate agent's windows.

Bad park
The park where there are no poop-scooping rules, so the two of you end up with dog shit up to your calves, and a hoodie who should not be riding his bike on the path in the first place cycles by and swipes the lady date's handbag.

Some parks are microcosms of how life can go wrong. All you need do is end up on a park bench listening to a tramp repeat the story of how he met this woman and she was a cow and he had a little drink and the next thing she was in a hostel with the kids and now his address is second bench along just under the beech tree.

Theatre trip

What can go wrong with a nice theatre trip? Nothing as long as you play safe and stick to a West End musical. *Chicago* is good as it has great tunes, a proper story (rare for a musical), plus lots of torn stocking and legs-akimbo chorus dancing for him. Also, lots of ladies of a certain age get hot under the collar about an ex-soap star making a triumphant return in this production – big names have recently included David Hasselhoff and Tony Hadley.

Don't go experimental and don't attempt foreign dance (it will involve nudity and strobe lighting, which could end up with your date fitting with an erection). Fringe theatre can be awkward as it often involves bad language, bad acting and really uncomfortable seats.

Going to see some comedy at a local pub will also be an unwise idea for the freshly courting middle-aged couple. You will be twenty years older than the rest of the audience and some idiot with a microphone will try and take the piss out of you. His 'banter' will include a great deal of sexual innuendo about anal sex, both of you will want to die of embarrassment, and the lady date will be a bit miffed that the man date didn't have the gumption to jump on stage and knock the blighter's lights out.

Dinner

Tricky one. This involves no other entertainment than eating and talking, and it can also be very costly – hmm, what to do? Avoid anywhere that involves picking things off a moving conveyor belt. Remember chopsticks lead to disaster and any establishment that doesn't do cutlery in any shape or form is a complete no-no. I will always remember my mother taking my father, who was in his sixties, for his very first McDonald's. Apparently he just stood there very disorientated with his tray of nuggets asking, 'Where are the knives and forks?'

You can do cheap as long as it's ironic and the food is good.

There are still a couple of cafés dotted about that do chips better than the Dorchester, but remember, men, a middle-aged woman , unless she has an overactive thyroid, will always be watching her weight. This is why it's your duty to order chips. Even if you don't want them, she will – just a couple, mind.

Even if she hoovers everything off the plate in record time, never say, 'I like a woman who enjoys her food.' She will hear. 'Alright porker, had enough yet or will it be a kebab on the way home as well?'

Italian is always a good option. It's the cheapest and least likely to lead to allergies. There is nothing worse than a pleasant evening ending in diarrhoea.

Cinema

The trouble with going to the cinema is that there is such a divide between man films and woman films. Ideally men should go to the cinema with men and see anything with the words *Bourne Identity* in the title, and women should go to the cinema with their chums to see that nice James McAvoy in that thing about Jane Austen. Unfortunately, dating rules mean that men have to try not to laugh or snore while watching stupid rom-coms like *The Holiday* while his lady date seethes beside him thinking, 'He must reckon I'm brain dead to enjoy this crap.'

The main problem with movies (amongst a great many other things) is that men and women do not share a sense of humour. Men like jokes with proper punch lines, watching cars crash and people falling over. Women are a lot more subtle and sophisticated. We like people saying funny and surprisingly clever things, and we tend to like our comedy slightly more cerebral. That said, we also like seeing people falling over – but only if it's a younger prettier woman.

One of the biggest problems with going to a see a movie when you are freshly dating is sitting through the rude bits. What are you meant to do? Should you join in and do a bit of snogging and writing along or should you shut your eyes, stick your fingers in your ears and go 'lalalalala' till it's over?

Of course the best thing about going to the cinema with a potential new partner is that you can tell a great deal about him/her by their cinema habits. If he has to buy hot dogs and tortilla crisps, he's a slob. However, if he has two secret cartons of Ribena in his pocket that he's brought from home, he's a tight arse. While watching the film, keep an eye on him. If he laughs at all the stupid bits, he's an idiot, if he has to keep asking you what's going on, he's an idiot and, finally, if he thinks Jennifer Lopez is a really good actress, he's an idiot.

On the other hand, if you're a fellow taking a lady out and she can't stop crying during the movie, watch it. She's probably a bit mad.

NB. Going to see anything that can be classed as pornographic on a first date is really stupid, unless you're a couple of filthy old swingers of course, in which case good luck to you.

DATING WHEN OLDER

How far to go on a first date and beyond

OK, you've done the cinema, the dinner and a little innocent hand holding. It's time to move things on – you're consenting adults after all, albeit consenting adults with cellulite, stretch marks and werewolf-like hairiness. At some point, you are going to have to navigate the pitch and putt of the metaphorical game of crazy golf that is sex.

I think you have to be a lot more careful now. Once you're over forty you can't do sex on the first night – that would be desperate, wouldn't it? What a middle-aged whore you would be. I think you'd have to wait till about the sixth. Was that too soon?
JENNY ECLAIR

So you might as well get yourself organised. Buy some new underwear and get on with it. Now that you are (very) grown up, either one of you can make the first sexual move – so you might as well pluck up courage and work out how you are going to lure them into your cunning little trap.

Asking someone 'back for coffee' – clearly this is nothing to do with coffee and all to do with making them know that you want to leap into bed with them ... But again, make sure you have done some preparation before you leave home in the first place.

Be prepared, set the scene

Good things to be strewn around the bathroom or bedroom are very small pants (even if you have never worn them), sex manuals (entirely unread), and expensive perfume bottles and labels (although this might be too subtle unless you are a lesbian).

If you are a man, avoid a cat litter tray with cat poo in, or indeed a cat full stop. The contents of your fridge can be critical: Tupperware is a very bad sign, especially if you have never been married, as she will assume your mother comes round a lot to do the ironing. Also beware posters, photos of self, photos of ex's, a preference for National Trust calendars or cuddly toys in a women. This would be a definite turn-off. An over-abundance of football paraphernalia might be a problem, as well as too many beer cans or empty wine bottles.

Keep it safe

For God's sake, play safe. I'm not just talking about condoms here, I'm talking about doing it in a nice bed with a properly sprung mattress. You are too old to be doing it on the floor. Not only are carpet burns a bad look, but these days a lot of people have laminated wooden flooring, which is a complete no-no for the mature lover as you will end up skidding all over the place.

If you are very nervous, more alcohol might seem like a good idea. Whiskey might seem terribly sophisticated but if you've been on the Chardonnay all night and you've a nervous tum the combination could prove lethal. There is nothing worse than a grown woman vomiting because she had too much to drink.

Men can also suffer in the downstairs department if they drink too much, which is acutely embarrassing because the woman will always think that it's because he doesn't fancy her, and why should he if she's been throwing up whiskey and Chardonnay onto his bathroom floor?

So, if you are going to go for a nightcap, why not have something hot and milky – say Horlicks or Ovaltine? Pros: this will relax you. Cons: you might relax to the point where both of you conk out on the sofa.

Music – yes or no

Music is quite useful as it can mask any extraneous noises, such as groaning bedsprings and joint clicking. Stick to something that isn't going to go too fast. You don't want to have to try and keep up and get all out of puff.

A bit of unthreatening classical music is probably best. Avoid military marching bands, weird seventies electronic pop or Chas & Dave.

Putting on the telly
This is bad.

Lighting
Candlelight is by far the most flattering but both of you, being the age you are, will be worried about the flammability of the duvet. If you are undecided as to whose house to go back to, choose whoever has a dimmer switch in the bedroom. Other options are to throw your knickers over the bedside light or pretend to be a bit kinky and blindfold him.

You could opt for a complete blackout, but then when it's all over one of you will want to go to the loo. If you can't see where you're going there is a distinct possibility that you might end up weeing in his wardrobe. This is a bad thing. Perhaps the best option then is to go for the complete blackout but keep a torch handy just in case.

Smells and noises
You will be worried about your breath. This is entirely natural and one of the reasons why Marks & Spencer's do a very strong mint – keep a tin in your handbag. You might also be worried about your tummy making that growling noise that it does when you get peckish in the night. If this happens, pretend you are growling in a sexy jungle-cat kind of way. Then, when he's finally fallen asleep, nip downstairs and find a biscuit.

Finally, farting. It might happen and sometimes not from the end you would expect it to come from. You have two choices here. You can a) die of shame or b) pretend it's amusing and laugh. If you go for b), try not to get hysterical. It frightens them

Grooming before doing it

Trimming the undercarriage area with a pair of nail scissors is fine – just don't get carried away. Middle-aged women with Brazilians are weird once you're past thirty: it's reptilian and wrong.

Don't take out your contact lenses, your chicken fillets and your teeth all in one go. Try and retain a little mystery. And bear in mind that you cannot make love in a pair of Marks & Spencer's minimiser control pants. They are going to have to come off at some point and, if it's going to be a struggle, do it behind locked doors.

Morning after a one-night stand: what to do

Even Grumpy Old People who are back in the dating game, or God forbid doing something hideous like getting off with someone when their partner isn't looking, are potentially one-night standers. OK, it's unlikely, but it does happen, in which case get up very, very early. This is the kindest way for everyone – for the person in bed and the person getting up. Unless you know someone very well, or are completely and utterly besotted with them (neither of which are likely to apply with a one-night stand), it is best to avoid one another altogether in the morning. There is nothing trickier than trying to make polite conversation with someone over a bowl of breakfast cereal when either a) you think they were the most hideous sexual mistake you have ever made in your life or b) you are worried that your boyfriend will come back home from the airport a tad early – or both. No – surely the best thing to do with one-night stands is to somehow or other make it home at night in a taxi before you are seen with eye shadow all over your cheeks, no nightwear for dressing to walk to the bathroom in, all the wrong clothes on in the morning, and the hideously cruel morning light has come storming through the curtains.

Of course, one of the advantages of being old – apart from having no shame left – is that we tend to forget stuff very easily. So, if you do end up doing something a bit silly, don't give yourself a hard time. By tomorrow you won't even remember what it was that you have a horrible feeling you might have done.

And, anyway, we all need a little bit of love now and again.

Basically, what this book is trying to say is don't worry. As our grandmothers used to say, 'It'll work its way out in the wash' – whatever that means!

LOVE IS

Were you to ask me for the best way to somebody's heart, I would say, 'Make yourself useful.' MATTHEW PARRIS

The most romantic thing Geof's done for me is that he will pick me up from an airport at four o'clock in the morning – without whining, without moaning. Just being there at the Arrivals when I arrive back at four or five o'clock in the morning. He is there, he is smiling, that's romantic. JENNY ECLAIR